W9-BWY-649

CLICK & CLOSE

CLICK & CLOSE

E-Nabling The Real Estate Transaction

John Tuccillo, Ph.D., CAE
James F. Sherry

**Real Estate
Education Company®**
A Kaplan Professional Company

While a great deal of care has been taken to provide accurate and current information, the ideas, suggestions, general principles and conclusions presented in this text are subJect to local, state, and federal laws and regulations, court cases, and any revisions of same. The reader is thus urged to consult legal counsel regarding any points of law—this publication should not be used as a substitute for competent legal advice.

Vice President: Carol L. Luitjens
Executive Editor: Diana Faulhaber
Project Manager: Ronald J. Liszkowski
Art Manager: Lucy Jenkins

Published by Real Estate Education Company,®
a division of Dearborn Financial Publishing, Inc.®

Printed in the United States of America

00 01 02 10 9 8 7 6 5 4 3 2

ISBN No. 0-7931-3636-9

Sherry, Jim.
    Click and close : e-nabling the real estate transaction /
    Jim Sherry, John Tuccillo
        p.cm.
    Includes index.
    ISBN 0-7931-3636-9
    1. Real estate business—Computer network resources—
United States.   2. Internet (Computer network)—United States.
I. Title.   II. Tuccillo, John A.
    HD255.S54   1999   99-045428
    025.06'33333 21—dc21   CIP

DEDICATION

This book is dedicated with great love and appreciation to our mothers, Mary Grace Sherry and Anna Tuccillo.

CONTENTS

Jim Sherry is a recognized authority on the real estate industry and widely sought for his visionary views on the industry's future. He is president of Innovative Solutions, Inc., a firm providing consulting services to major real estate enterprises, real estate franchises, and top technology firms serving the real estate industry.

Mr. Sherry's background is in computer technology at NCR Corporation and RCA, where he held positions in computer system design and software development. He was formerly president and CEO of Interealty Corp., a computer services and publishing company and the market leader in MLS systems.

Jim is a popular speaker, giving over thirty speeches a year to gatherings of every segment of the real estate industry.

John Tuccillo is the leading economist in the real estate industry and recognized as a leading thinker on the future of real estate. His book, *The Eight New Rules of Real Estate,* released in 1998, has become one of the best-selling real estate books ever published.

From 1987 to 1997, Dr. Tuccillo was chief economist for the NATIONAL ASSOCIATION OF REALTORS®, and prior to that the chief economist at the National Council of Savings Institutions (now America's Community Bankers). He holds a doctorate in economics from Cornell University and an undergraduate degree from Georgetown University.

John is a sought after speaker in the areas of economics, real estate, and technology. His presentations are invariably witty, informative, and understandable. In addition, he has facilitated numerous strategic planning efforts for nonprofit and other companies.

ACKNOWLEDGMENTS

No book can ever be done alone. The ideas need to be organized, turned into prose, prepared, reviewed, and ultimately debated for content, insight, and effect. We have been the beneficiaries of a great deal of help. Tony Ciepel, Dick Purvis, and Michele Wiegand shared with us their insights about the real estate business. Jim Beckham, Bob Boyd, and Tom Matthes provided the benefit of their creativity and experience to ground this book in the reality of the real estate market. Kate Anderson provided the transcription of the tapes that are the basis for the book and performed her customary superlative editing job. Kelly Raider and Addie Staebler prepared the manuscript and diligently tracked down our references. Our thanks to all of them for their contributions.

The New Rules Revisited

TWELVE MONTHS IS MORE THAN A YEAR

Last year, John Tuccillo wrote about the eight new rules of real estate. They were designed to outline the thinking necessary to respond to the pressures of the marketplace and to evolve from the current business model of real estate to one that could succeed in the new world. At the time the book began circulating, the rules appeared to be ahead of practice. The industry, at the beginning of the third record-breaking year in a row, was doing quite well. As 1999 unfolded, it was clear that existing home sales would spend most of the year at rates above 5 million and that the only problems with homebuilding were in supply, not demand. The industry did not have time to endure the pain of change.

But around the fringes of the industry the status quo was most definitely threatened. Firms from outside the industry—companies that already played by the rules or were too new to know any other way—were changing the way the business was done.

Technology firms, noticing the great labor intensity of the industry, saw the opportunity to squeeze profit out of the business by increasing operational efficiency. Their models—travel agencies, insurance companies, full-service brokerage firms, and others—already had proven the gains to be made, and real estate looked like the next likely target. Companies from outside the industry either bought in, or were already in and attempted to link household-related services to get more of each customer's business.

Additionally, a number of vendors were attempting to market to the industry software tools that would automate the current process in a way that would allow real estate firms to capture more of the cash flow generated by each transaction. These tools allowed the mortgage, title, appraisal, and settlement functions to be handled by a single central source for a set fee and thus freed licensees to handle customers more intensively.

So, in 1999 we saw the integration of neighborhood data, mortgage information, and household services links on Microsoft's Home Advisor, Home Store's REALTOR.COM, and Cyber Homes. We saw GMAC acquire Better Homes and Gardens, and Mid-America Power expand its holdings of real estate firms. From outside the business, Home Bid, Ellie Mae, iProperty, and Real Estate.com led the charge to automate part or all of the real estate transaction. In the year since *The Eight New Rules of Real Estate* was published, the market has become exceedingly crowded with products and services that offer nothing less than the complete reinvention of the real estate transaction.

Despite all this (or maybe because of it), the movement of traditional real estate firms to a new model based on the new rules has been slow. Instead, an awareness that the industry was changing in the direction of the rules spread rapidly accompanied by the anxious feeling that how to get there was unclear. In part, the swift entrance into the market of new firms and new products has confused the need for and direction of change for the typical firm. The analogy is the consumer who sees more powerful and less expensive personal computers on the market each week and then cannot choose, fearing that any move is the wrong one.

That feeling was valid. *The Eight New Rules of Real Estate* issued a clarion call about change, its speed, and the scope of the challenges facing those in the real estate industry. This book addresses the implementation question. It attempts to lay out the process by which you can equip your business to be successful into the future. It is a blueprint for creating the systems that will make you competitive in a world where information flows freely and virtually without cost, where competitors can crop up from anywhere at any time, and where the market is directed by the buyer instead of the seller.

Using this book to reinvent your business does not require that you have read about the eight new rules; references to *The Eight New Rules of Real Estate* are few and are largely self-contained. But it is good to have at least a passing understanding of what the rules are.

THE RULES

Without going into great detail, the new rules are presented below.

General Rules

1. **Your business is global whether or not you sell beyond the boundaries of your town.**
2. **Speed to market is everything.**
3. **You'll never walk alone. Business is done through strategic alliances.**
4. **Abandon your successes quickly.**

Specific Rules

1. **The most powerful economic unit is the individual.** Market power has shifted from the supplier to the consumer of goods and services, and business models in varied industries—including real estate— have been shattered as a result.
2. **Lock the customer in for life by creating unique value.** There is no more consumer loyalty; business goes where the most value is created, and the continuing creation of value (and only that) will attract the customer.

3. **The middle is disappearing.** The market will no longer reward those who convey information without adding value to it. Real estate is an information business and, like travel agencies, full-service brokerages, and others, is in real danger of disappearing.

4. **Think content.** The successful firm of the future will be one filled with knowledge workers. This means a company where information is turned into knowledge (i.e., made actionable) for the benefit of the consumer. Information is free; knowledge is priceless.

5. **Mine your bits.** The information available to the typical real estate professional about his or her clients and customers is the basis for the creation of marketing profiles of great value. It will allow the targeting of customers as well as the provision of extraordinary service to them.

6. **Sell the experience, not the product.** Branding is essential in modern business, and there are no brands in real estate. Doing it the same way every time, so that the consumer can count on a satisfactory experience every time, is the basis of branding.

7. **Feed the OODA (observe, orient, decide, and act) loop.** Providing continuing value to the consumer requires knowing what the consumer values. This requires being close to your market and regularly sensing those needs.

8. **Know what business you're in.** Real estate has little to do with structures and land. It has everything to do with information. The job of the real estate professional is to broker information about property for sale, and to do it using systems that provide completely satisfactory results every time.

These rules were adapted from the changes that were occurring in business in general. They are not optional, except for those with short time horizons and no desire to build for the long-term. They have emerged as technology has changed the way in which information is treated, and in doing so nullified the power of current business models to guarantee success in the future.

USING THE RULES FOR SUCCESS

Success is easy now because economic conditions are such that merely working hard will ensure profit. But in the future, the economy and the housing market will slow. And new generations of consumers, accustomed to wireless communication and freely available information, will come to dominate the market. Then it will be impossible to survive without using the new rules to pattern your business.

Nor will the pace of change slow. Consumers are becoming better equipped, more knowledgeable, and generally more powerful in wielding the technology tool to exert their desires in the market. We have always had new technologies and consumers have always had to climb the learning curve to use these technologies. Well, those learning curves now have built-in escalators.

Adapting to these rules is not an easy task. Company culture will dictate how fast and how far you can drive the model. More important, your own capabilities and resources will either propel you into the future or anchor you to the past.

- At the very least you must learn to be comfortable with technology. Real estate professionals have grown into everything from fax machines to cell phones; they will soon grow into electronic commerce. Those who don't have the ability to keep up with the pace of change in information technology and don't see how using these developments can positively alter their future will fall behind in the competition for consumer loyalty.
- Information is the currency of the past; knowledge is the currency of the future. You need to fill your bank account. Playing by the rules means the ability to take

information and make it actionable for the consumer. This requires an understanding of where information is, how to access it, and how to use it to meet consumer needs.

- The rules work best when you combine them with knowledge of where your market is going. Economic conditions are important, but they are primarily short-term. More important is a reading of the longer-term trends. This means knowing how the demographic and employment trends of your market area are evolving, and how technology is affecting the way your market-place works. Market foresight is a product of dedication and discipline; developing it requires that you set aside some real thinking time.

- Capital is necessary now as it has never been before in the real estate business. With the revolution in information technology, the price of doing business has gone up. Creating a system that delivers consumer satisfaction requires integrated technology. This is a competency that the real estate business does not possess. It must be purchased, as must be the hardware and software to run the system. All this requires capital resources.

- The system itself should produce customer satisfaction in the same way every time. This means automating information flow in a fast, easy manner, while employing skilled professionals to use knowledge to create consumer value. Currently, real estate professionals spend a great deal of time managing clients, inventory, and transactions. All those tasks can be managed more efficiently and in a more consistent manner automatically through the system, freeing time for value creation.

- People will always be the backbone of the real estate industry, but the mix of talents needed in the industry will of necessity change. Licensees will concentrate on designing the answers to their clients needs, while routine tasks will be handled by customer service representatives whose competencies will include ease with people and technological savvy. In turn, management will face different challenges, as new personnel policies will be needed to handle the new mix of people.

All of these rules revert to one of the basic general rules: You'll never walk alone. In every one of them, partnering or strategic alliances represent either the least costly or only route to attaining success. As you go through this book, you will see the rules in action. More important, you will see the planning necessary to implement the rules and move your business into the future.

We are often asked how many real estate professionals will be needed in the future. The answer may be fewer or it may be the same number, doing different things. But one thing is clear: Unless you can reinvent your business to meet the demands of the market, whatever number of real estate professionals exist will be one fewer.

REALTORS® in the New World of Business

THE STORY OF JOHN AND MARY JACKSON

Long before the Bose® Wave® radio fills the room with warm music to wake up to, the vital signs of John and Mary's home are monitored constantly by a computer. This modern safety net is in addition to the roving patrols and the gated pathways leading in and out of the subdivision. John, a REALTOR®, wanted a family protection policy of sorts, just as he had sought out good teachers and modern classrooms for his two kids. Over the years, he's seen the slow migration from the city to the outer limits of the county, which was once the home of ranchers and grazing cattle. Here, developers have created enclaves with virtually every good and service nearby. And, with the steady advance of technology, electronics, and machines, people are quickly in touch with each other, although good personal relationships seem more and more rare.

The smell of rich coffee wafts upward from the kitchen, bringing a smile across John's unshaven face. He gives Mary, his wife of 20 years, a slight nudge. She stumbles into the bathroom, and after a quick brush of the teeth and stroke of the hair, heads down the hallway to begin the usual 15-minute ritual of getting their two children—Cindy, 13 and Rob, 10—out of bed and ready for school. Mary takes time to check the computer screen staring out from the desk across from their bed, making sure the kids' homework assignments from the night before were completed. The Jacksons are part of a pilot study begun by the school system about a year ago, one grateful result of higher taxes. It brings parents, teachers, and students closer together, overcoming—electronically—lost opportunities to communicate due to helter-skelter schedules and the interminable absentmindedness of the kids themselves. Not only can John and Mary know precisely the homework assignments, but through e-mail they can keep track of Cindy and Rob's progress, as well as the long and complicated schedule of school events.

In the mornings the kids are eerily quiet, a contrast with what seems like ADD behavior during the rest of their 14-hour days. How on earth do they do it? Mary thinks. Work a math problem, talk on the telephone, watch television, and—for a break—turn to the latest handheld video game. The more she ponders, however, the more Mary sees her kids' lives as a reflection of the family's daily obligations—not that much different than the other two-income families who live on Quail Ridge Drive.

The Jacksons, like a hefty majority of Americans, need a dual stream of dollars to surround themselves with life's necessities and add in some pleasures when they have the time. This is not how it was supposed to be. When Mary and John were in college, academic and government sages were predicting a shortened workweek, more leisure time, and early retirement on a pension gained through years of service to the same company. Mary's first job included an orientation program that mapped out her career path, complete with a chart of expected earnings and benefits.

For a variety of reasons, precisely the opposite happened. Great corporate names of just two decades ago are, as someone put it, "bugs on a windshield," gone to mergers, acquisitions, and bankruptcy. The concept of work also has been radically altered. An eight-hour day at a central office with a supervisor holding forth is more and more antique. Large corporations are sending their charges home, giving them more personal responsibility while cutting way down on overhead. Corporate America is embracing the entrepreneurial spirit—a trait that always characterized the real estate business. Selling property is intensely personal, most always hinging on the ability to connect one person with another. In a longer view, however, working is not the same as it used to be.

Instead of the neatly packaged and predictable world in which John and Mary's parents had prospered, today's work environment is fragmented and dispersed. It's the same on the home front. Something as routine as feeding the family is monitored by a computer program networked into a local supermarket. Check the inventory, punch in the new items, and have them delivered the same day.

A casual look at the daily obligations on the computer in the kitchen reveals the real world the Jacksons live in. The schedule includes karate for Rob and dance for Cindy (on alternative days of the week) in addition to the social and athletic demands of the moment at their school. These outside endeavors tend to be seasonal and faddish, as the occasion might warrant. There never seems to be enough time to fit it all in—in addition to the full-time and demanding jobs of each parent, and their attempts to take a breather at the theater and in an occasional round of golf.

Even with all the doodads that festoon the kitchen, the Jacksons' first meal of the day is usually the ultimate experience in fast food. The kids seem to take the occasion to bellyache about school food, as have generations of students before them. John, for his part, usually gulps down some coffee and stops for a low-cal snack at the Jiffy Mart half way to his office. In the early mornings, parents with kids in tow head to the full range of academic gradations—from preschool to senior high. Seen from a satellite's piercing eye, Quail Ridge Drive, and millions of suburban streets just like it, look like time-lapse photography with objects spurting in and out, lights flashing on and off, and people moving like ants leaving a mound.

Back on earth, John adjusts his lanky frame into the downy confines of leather upholstery inside his dark blue four-door automobile. This particular model has a special link to a roving satellite, which sends signals about the car's critical operating parts to a central receiving station. In effect, the system actually diagnoses trouble before it happens, and lets the driver know when a trip to the dealer is needed. It also has a location wizard that can direct John to his destination, in plain steps like those books "for dummies."

There is something almost reverential about the automobile in America and especially to the lives of REALTORS®. The car always was more than transportation. It was part of the REALTOR®'s personality and a piece of the presentation to prospective buyers. Early in John's career, carting new home-seekers around was a good deal like taking a lazy walk in the countryside. There was time to snail through newly paved streets, wandering about until something caught the prospect's eye.

Now, of course, the data that had previouly been doled out to customers by REALTORS® is in the public domain through the Internet—and a prospect a thousand miles away can take a virtual walk through a property on a CRT. This is as bizarre as the ability to flick on a cellular phone, reach anyone in the world in a flash, read e-mail, and get messages that were left when the owners were unavailable. These changes have come slowly, yet they seem to have appeared overnight. John, Mary, and their children are conditioned to this high-tech world, lifting their expectations for precision and speed to heights they never imagined.

John's car is a car in name only. It's an electronic marvel packaged in a combination of mostly plastics and aluminum. Its huge engine is stingy with gasoline (the high-octane variety of course) and is computer-driven from stem to stern. Most of its safety and performance packages are the result of changing social tastes and also core values about lifestyle and environmental quality. John's car need not get a tune-up for 100,000 miles, and before too long he may not change his engine oil over the car's operating life. The car is in constant communication with the service center so that when John takes it to the dealer, computers overseen by a technician have already "read" its internal organs, diagnosed any deficiencies, and prepared the necessary remedies.

John's usual trip to the office follows a well-traveled four-lane arterial where fast-food stores and service stations are the rule. As is his practice, John wheels into a service center about two miles from his home that's been transformed in the past five years from a gasoline station to what is now called a "codevelopment" outlet. At this multipurpose way station, there's an ATM, a fast-food outlet, a retail groceries section, a dry-cleaning shop, bays for oil changing, a car wash, and a computer screen that offers the daily news as the driver fills up. John pays for his fuel by passing a small electronic capsule across the face of the gas pump. Why all these services in the same place? Because it is impossible for such businesses to survive without many income streams coming from multiple goods and services. It's also impossible to drive such a business onward in this changing world unless one goes faster and faster just to keep from falling behind.

Mary Jackson, who earned a degree in business and went on to complete a master's degree shortly after she and John were married, is the quintessential model of the modern woman. Her devotion to her family is second only to her deep desire to get ahead professionally. A few years ago, Mary was approached by an old friend who was entering a totally foreign and uncharted field that reached consumers directly through the World Wide Web. She had only scarcely heard of e-commerce, but the idea of pioneering and the possibility of high rewards appealed to her competitive spirit. Now, e-commerce is on every lip and every mind in the business world. E-commerce stocks, including her own company's, are skyrocketing upward.

Mary is wowed by the unstructured way she and her growing contingent go about business. There are no hard and fast rules of engagement. Sure, there are some fundamental operating procedures that all businesses need to have. She had once heard this new approach called "stability in motion." But in the main, this brood flies by the seat of their jeans. Risks abound. Mary is mindful that a larger company may swoop down and gobble up her venture. But so what? As a shareholder she's likely to benefit handsomely, and she'll use the experience as a stepping stone to another, perhaps even more profitable, enterprise.

Mary is confident that learning and planning strategy as you go are the models for success in hectic times that are laced with huge potential. The thought of coming to work excites her. That she is in command of her own fate is uplifting. And the sense of individual accomplishment and contribution in an atmosphere that also promotes teamwork is satisfying. So, Mary's days are always filled with new challenges. She and her team are resigned to the new and different and excited by the opportunity to learn and ride the wave where it takes them. Or better, where they are able to steer their ship riding the wave.

As John pulls off the highway and heads toward his office, he's already made good use of his cell phone—one of the tools that have long served the real estate profession. The difference is in the technology, but the purpose is the same—to put him in touch with new customers and to serve the needs of those who have chosen him to represent their interests.

As John steps from his car, his cell phone signals an incoming message. He smiles broadly as he learns the deal he is proposing is done. All that's left now is to get the buyer through the process. John enters the room, speaks to the receptionist, grabs another cup of coffee, and glides over to his desk. He picks out a contract, sticks it into a 20-year-old electric typewriter, and begins to fill it out.

CHAPTER 1

Catching the Wave

The major challenge facing residential real estate today is the need for reinvention of the real estate firm from the current model to the future business model in the face of a large portion of the industry that simply doesn't want to go there.

—Anthony M. Ciepel, President and Chief Operating Officer, Realty One

The contrast between John's professional world and the larger world around him is remarkable. It isn't that John is lazy or unconcerned; nor is he against change. The real issue for John, and millions of others in the real estate field, is how best to exploit the enormous potential that is offered by the revolutionary change in information technology and the tools that are so much a part of this new dynasty. This is not new stuff. Shakespeare wrote that a new tide in the affairs of men leads to fortune but warned we must catch the wave at its uppermost point, or face the consequences. The message rings true for all of us in the real estate industry. We need to see change as a friend, without fear. A new wave of operations doesn't require that any of us be pioneers. Yet, we need to catch up to the wave if we are to thrive in a new world of competition.

There's an old saw that explores the paradox of time: "Those who have money have no time," it goes "and, those who have time have no money." The John's and Mary's of this world are caught somewhere in-between. Their time is more precious, even as their need for money grows to provide the goods and services that make their time worthwhile. The constant pressures have changed their outlook about how their time is used.

Think about it. In every nook and cranny of our lives we are demanding the best, and we expect those who supply us with goods and services to jump through more hoops every year. If you don't like the interest rate offered by a bank or credit card company, shop around. Getting your car serviced, a mundane chore that carries a relatively low price tag, used to be one of those hit-or-miss propositions that depended on the good nature and schedule of a mechanic. Now, an appointment is made with a personal service manager at the car dealer who will follow up with you to ensure that you received an outstanding and satisfying experience. Companies that are focused on customer service are the ones riding waves of fortune.

It's our strong belief that the real estate industry has yet to see the wave, let alone ride it. The real estate business model is old fashioned, and industry professionals are being left behind.

Sure, REALTORS® and their customers are up to speed on the technological tools of the trade. Take the evolution of the telephone—from the rotary dial to the cell-phone age. We have seen the instrument change and the terms of service become chaotic. We have the opportunity to both choose any long distance supplier and select from a cornucopia of phone styles and colors sold on virtually every corner. Venerable AT&T is now one of many telephone service competitors. Its brain trust, Bell Labs, is now Lucent Technologies, knocking the socks off the stock market. Cell phones are like appendages to most Americans, whether it's the teenager at school or the hardhat at a construction site. For REALTORS®, the cell phone is an opportunity to store and retrieve information, send and receive e-mail, and in some models, serve as an intercom. The same comparisons apply to virtually every tool at the REALTORS®' command—fax machines, copiers, and of course the personal computer.

A REALTOR®'s information delivery systems have evolved steadily over the past quarter century—from loose-leaf to books to thermal printers to plain-paper printers to computers on a desktop and now to laptop computers that can be uploaded and downloaded over cell phones and through satellite networks. "Modern" Mary Jackson is living in this virtual world at home *and* at her office. Mary can exchange information and communicate with clients via computer from her desk. "Jurassic" John and millions of his peers are manually trekking hard copy from one office to another, assembling reams of paper by hand, and running a sequential signing marathon to finish a transaction. What's wrong with this picture?

Look across the business landscape and you'll find that information is a powerful customer service tool. It's steadily captured in digital form, stored, compiled, compared, and used for years to profile and service customers who are enriched with information that's freely available on the Internet. Businesses are turning information into knowledge that is used to get and keep customers for life, and this helps them to thrive.

Take something as mundane as an oil change. Pop in, give the attendant your $30, and pop out within 10 or 15 minutes. Behind the pressurized car lifters and the repetitive routine of the workers, is a database that tells operators your whims, your buying habits, your product tastes, and tracks your whereabouts from one location to the next. If you do move and have a buying history, you'll get a reminder by mail about every three months. The fast-lube business isn't just selling motor oil anymore. These businesses are pushing full service—taking over the tasks that used to be the province of the local service station. All this is involved in a $30 piece of business.

Compare the oil lube with selling a home that costs in the thousands of dollars, and is often the single largest investment a family will make. Instead of using stored information as fuel to drive our future economic engine, we dutifully rid ourselves of this great resource. Instead of housing the information in a sophisticated computer database, we stick paper files in a steel cabinet, without much (if any) intention of picking them up again.

Let's go back to the oil change for a moment. In the "Do It for Me" market, as it's known in the trade, the goal is far more than keeping an engine humming smoothly. The consumer is easily connected to dozens of other products and services, including an array of choices offered by credit card companies.

Clearly, real estate presents an incomparable opportunity to leverage more consumer information and connect those buyers to far more products and services. We're talking about 5.5 million real estate transactions a year. Those transactions take place on commodities—on products—on objects that are costing $150,000 each in the marketplace, and in which each transaction allows you to link two different households.

This should be a wake-up call for every real estate professional. Our industry is gold to be mined. The pump of innovation is primed. The question is who are going to step up and be the leaders, the innovators in our industry? We don't know who you are, but we do know the steps you can take to change your business life.

Before we get to the answers, keep this picture in your mind. The business world is a great deal like a solar system. The planets, the various pieces of our business, are constantly moving in different orbits. They change with the seasons, according to their own location in space.

THE ROLE OF THE INTERNET

At the center of this business "solar system" is the World Wide Web, a colossus of data that feeds information through all parts of the universe—an energy source without boundaries or limitations. Like the sun, the Web pulsates, feeding on itself to produce even more energy. The Web is so crucial, so profound, precisely because information is our greatest capital asset. Natural resources no longer are needed for a nation to achieve greatness. Instead of precious metals or oil, brain-power is the force that drives success. The Internet is the key that starts that engine.

But the Internet turns virtually all of human history on its ear. Until the late Twentieth Century, control of information was power. Controlling information was the bulwark of the Soviet empire, which was able to build both physical and psychological walls to keep people in and ideas out. An assault by armed forces didn't bring down the Berlin Wall. The end actually began with the first satellite orbiting in space. In less than thirty years, information fed through this hardware and the magic of television opened the eyes of Soviet Bloc peoples to the world around them. It was impossible for the state to blot out the peoples' desire for personal freedom and economic prosperity generated by knowledge of how the rest of the world really lived. The Soviet people wanted a piece of the pie, and they grabbed for it.

Compared to the information channels that helped to destroy the Soviet empire, the Internet's power to store and deliver information is light years ahead. It's beyond anything else in our lifetime, and it's gaining strength each day. And it is not an overstatement to say that comparing the Internet today to the Internet tomorrow is like comparing the biplane to the Starship Enterprise.

What do REALTORS® think of the Internet? Studies show that real estate professionals use its power far less than the average American does. Far too many REALTORS® see the Internet as a threat to business, much as the Luddites of the Industrial Revolution saw the steam engine as a destroyer of their way of life.

The Industrial Revolution was the greatest boon to jobs and economic growth and development the world had ever known. The Internet has the same kind of pent-up power. There are good reasons to see it as a friend and neighbor.

- **The Internet is a great enabler for all business.** It's the ultimate knowledge warehouse. All information known to humanity is waiting to be tapped at anytime, anywhere, and can be communicated instantaneously through all information systems. The limitations on the Internet are not in information, they are in transmission speed.

- **The Internet is boundary-less.** The Internet renders geography meaningless. The old AT&T slogan, "Reach Out and Touch Someone" has a new meaning.

- **The Internet is a great equalizer.** There are no special qualifications or training needed to use this bank of knowledge. It does not discriminate on any basis. Indeed, the Internet is a catalyst to use products and services more capably and usefully.

- **The Internet is a great information liberator.** Anyone with the tools can tap into a "black hole" of data cooped up in computers all over the world. It's not simply analogous to the liberating force that brought down totalitarianism. Instead, the Internet opens the door of knowledge to all consumers—making ordinary people "instant" experts on a limitless number of topics and subjects. Want to learn more about a disease or a cure? Interested in the background and performance of stocks? Want to see what a car or appliance really costs? Interested in buying life insurance and want to choose from one hundred top companies? Want to buy or sell a home, rebuild a home, search for property, and find a REALTOR® to handle your business? The information is at your fingertips.

- **The Internet is a catalyst for more innovation and competition.** The Internet empowers consumers with knowledge and forces the other links in the marketing chain to grow stronger. Educated consumers demand more value, and intermediaries in any transaction are obligated to meet or exceed consumer expectations if they are to retain these customers. What is more, because consumers can get speedy access to information via the Internet, their appetite for speed, service, and value is applied to other goods and services traded in more traditional markets.

You can point to the Net as the catalyst that is forcing innovation in our business. For years, real estate operated under rules that the industry set and carried out. The Net has changed this, forever. The customer is privy to all of the once closely held data about taxes, location, and demographics, and has the inside track of comparative shopping. And, it's free.

The Internet is a challenging medium. It's a medium that ups the ante and causes you to react. You have a choice. You can convince yourself that the Internet is a passing fad. Or, you can embrace and use change to your advantage. When the first Spanish sail appeared over the horizon and the natives in Mexico saw it, they did nothing because sails were not a part of their consciousness. By doing nothing they allowed the conquistadores to come in, and a new, unfriendly world became reality. We believe a new world order in real estate is here, and it's past time for agents and brokers alike to make the best use of it. How to learn and prosper in this new world is what this book is about.

THE PLAN OF THIS BOOK

This book describes a new business model that can be adapted to cope with the changing market you face. In the remainder of this book, we will develop the dynamics of this new world of real estate.

- In Chapter 2, we'll look at how the real estate transaction and business structures are changing. Why is it undergoing a steady metamorphosis? Why is power flowing to consumers? Who are the new market entrants and what are the shifting roles within our business?
- In Chapter 3, we talk about how you can create what we call the "value proposition" for consumers. In other

words, how can you add value to the empowered consumer? The answer lies in developing a business model that helps create a more successful agent and broker.

- In Chapters 4 through 6, we pull together the pieces that comprise this new model: an effective strategic plan, a technology plan, and recruiting and training the team to get the job done.

- Chapter 7 provides a blueprint for building the new enterprise using technology, including an insider's view of how it's being done in one particular firm.

- In the final two chapters, we turn our attention to the goal of making the consumer a customer for life; a friend and confidant rather than a fleeting acquaintance. This is done by understanding the role of information, and by developing a system to capture, manage, and use information in your business to add value to the consumer.

As we make this journey together, a roadmap is needed to make sure we take the right turns and twists toward success. Throughout our lives all of us have approached the new and unsure with trepidation—with a lump in our throats. It's so easy to tackle life in the same comfortable way using the same tried and true methods. The problem is the world is moving much too fast for that kind of thinking anymore. It's true that a company needs to be ever more productive just to keep up with the competition. To be a leader, it has to show others the door on the way to higher earnings and growth. We are no different. The real estate industry is no different. Yet, real estate professionals have a tremendous advantage. The home is a precious commodity, whether it's for investment or sentimental value. Owning a home is the bedrock of political and economic freedom, principles cherished in our society. REAL-TORS® are the people who make these dreams become reality. With the right tools, and the right plans, you can travel this road swiftly, surely, and successfully.

2

The Changing Real Estate Business Environment

A mind once stretched by a new idea can never go back to its original dimensions.
—Oliver Wendell Holmes

INTRODUCTION

Back on Quail Ridge Drive, the Jacksons are a good example of how the world around them is changing, and how they, as people on the move, are influencing those changes. When John, Mary, and the kids go on vacation they use their online travel counselor, an electronic agent that bargains with hotels, airlines, and even sets up an itinerary for the trip. Their daily sustenance is provided in part by the local supermarket, clued into their wants by computer. In turn, the supermarket sends to the Jacksons the latest specials, even menus for the trying.

Working at home with their virtual bank, John and Mary use an electronic counselor to find out about mutual funds, IRAs, loans, and the myriad possibilities for handling their mundane financial transactions. They are not only conditioned to control, speed, and convenience, they demand it. Now that they have experienced the satisfaction of personal treatment, they aren't about to accept anything less.

It's no wonder why John's industry—real estate—is being pressured and pushed in the same directions. Real estate isn't an island, even if it might wish it was. External forces are pushing the industry to deliver services faster, cheaper, and better. Families searching for homes used to think of the real estate transaction as a single event. Now, it's seen as a series of subevents: the search for the home, the negotiating of a contract, the contact with the settlement service providers, the achievement of different settlement services, and finally, the closing itself. In addition, consumers increasingly see the housing transaction extending beyond the settlement. Once they are in their new home, owners turn to making their dwelling even better through refurbishing and renovating.

The changing real estate landscape has much to do with the way the new generation views it. The world of their children Rob and Cindy will be far different than John and Mary's. Generation X—and the generation that comes even later—see home ownership as a physical asset and attach far less sentiment to the transaction. This doesn't mean that Rob and Cindy won't want to do as their parents have done. But succeeding generations are far more transient. They live in a world in constant flux. Years ago, credit card companies routinely rejected applicants who changed jobs often. This was regarded as "instability." Now, job changing is the order of the day, and is viewed as a necessary and good stepping-stone to improvement.

The real estate industry is changing in four crucial ways:

1. The Internet is empowering consumers, raising their expectations, and (related to both) creating new competitors in the business.
2. Both the transaction and the business structure are changing, requiring a new efficiency in operations.
3. New entrants see real estate as a trillion-dollar business, and are attempting to enter it to gain a share of those revenues. This puts pressure on traditional real estate firms to approach business life more efficiently.
4. Within the traditional competitors, roles are shifting and there is a race to achieve the position of transaction manager.

This section examines the changes that are affecting the industry and the reasons for those changes. Finally, we look at how, in this new world, real estate firms can create the value proposition demanded by the market.

EMPOWERED CONSUMERS

The consumer movement began over four decades ago with Ralph Nader's campaign against General Motors. But Nader's Raiders and the like are essentially political, working at the grass roots to enable change; more often than not, legislative change. Power came from the aggregate strength of many people working together. In a number of cases, changes in laws and regulations forced businesses to make hard choices. Either they complied, moved into other fields, or got out of the business altogether. But the key concept here is that there were ways for firms to avoid dealing with consumer activists.

Now, consumerism is a different animal and there's no place to hide. Consumers no longer need the strength of a political movement. They need only the added strength that comes from access to a huge bank of information. Today's consumer is like Popeye, who gulps down a can of spinach, turns himself into a mini-Hercules, and saves Olive Oyl and the world. But the power source these days doesn't come out of a can, it comes out of a computer. The Internet is an egalitarian vehicle—dispossessing no one. The more consumers are attuned to the market, have intimate details about how things work and why they happen, the more easily they can master their choices. And, more significant, the more bargaining power they enjoy.

The knowledge that comes from the Internet is pervasive, affecting all who tap into it. The Internet makes the consumer information-rich, independent, and self-reliant. This means consumers don't show up, hats in hand, needing someone to shepherd them through every twist and turn of a business transaction. Quite the contrary, the Net eliminates entirely the old intermediary source in the market. The Internet has shifted market power from the hands of producers to those of consumers.

This shifting of market power from producers to consumers manifests itself in ways as small as the distribution of consumer time. John and Mary were once confined to the physical location and hours of operation of stores and banks to meet their shopping and banking needs. Even with expanded and Sunday hours, the restrictions still constrained their choices.

Now, with catalog sales, ATMs, and electronic commerce, consumer power is unfettered. This has placed a great deal of pressure on retail establishments and banks. They must match the speed and convenience of electronic transactions and then add additional value to differentiate themselves in the marketplace. So, retailers such as Wal-Mart and Nordstrom's thrive against the competition from catalogs and the Internet because they offer price and service value that make them superior options.

But consumption is only one aspect of the newly empowered consumer. Take the case of university professors. They were once restricted to whatever texts the publishers offered to them. Usually these were intended for the mass market and thus contained a great deal of irrelevant material. Now, professors can download specific articles from the Internet and "create" their own texts that contain only those materials they deem relevant to the specific courses they are teaching.

In the real estate industry, the empowered consumer now is a full participant—an active participant—in the transaction of buying and selling of real property. Consumers increasingly view the real estate transaction not as a single transaction but as a chain of sequential steps. That chain (see Figure 2.1) begins with the listing or prescreening of homes and ends with the final signatures at the settlement table. In between are the contract to buy or sell, the financing of the home, the title assurance, the home inspection, and any other pieces that

FIGURE 2.1 Decision to Buy/Sell

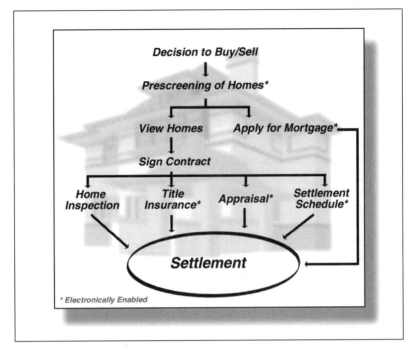

might be necessary to make the transaction happen. And, increasingly, each of these steps is coming under the direct control of the consumer.

Consumers today can visit real estate Web sites and look at virtually any available property. They can get a competitive market analysis from an outside Web site to determine when, how, and at what price to put their house on the market. They can go to a mortgage site and look at mortgage rates, determine the financial burden of alternative instruments, assess the potential value of refinancing, and apply for a loan on a new or existing home. They can go to title company Web sites and look at information on titles, to understand the title process a bit better, and also to decide what kind of title insurance they might want to have. They also can go to home insurance sites, apply for insurance on their new home, or reinsure the home they currently have. More importantly, several sites on the Internet are attempting to consolidate a number of these functions into a single action.

Further, even during the process, some Web sites allow the consumer to track the pace and progress of a transaction. So, at any juncture consumers can know how the system works, and where the roadblocks are in going to settlement. This ties back in to the view the consumer has—that the real estate transaction is a bundling of processes, instead of a single event and a single unit. The key is that the consumer is in control throughout, eliminating the need for an intermediary in the traditional sense.

None of this means that the real estate professional is going the way of the dinosaurs. Neither does it suggest that a person can't list, sell, mortgage, and title property independently. But consumers are going to take far more responsibility, and have a great deal more input in the home sales transaction. It does mean that the empowered consumer is causing an evolution of the role of the real estate intermediary. In the past, the intermediary created value simply by being there; by providing information that the consumer could not otherwise access. Now, the real estate intermediaries are being forced to demonstrate how they create value for the consumer.

"RAISE THE BAR COMPETITORS"

The real estate industry's structure is also in transition—in ownership, size, focus, and character. As in so many other industries, there's a rapid consolidation in the real estate industry. Virtually all the franchises have become more active in the marketplace, and every large independent firm is in an acquisition mode. Statistics suggest that consolidation is resulting in an increase in corporate size. The industry is evolving itself into a combination of large firms that include independents, public corporations, and some franchise operations, and small boutique firms that tend to exist in a very small and well-defined market niche.

But there are also silent competitors—ones that are not even in the real estate business—who are changing the structure of the business. These are firms that are training real estate customers to expect things faster, cheaper, and better. "Raise the bar competitors" means exactly what the phrase implies: Competitive levels will be raised by companies that are not in the real estate industry.

Conditioners

The first type of "raise the bar competitor" is the *conditioner.* John and Mary Jackson are conditioned to demand the same perks and accommodations in all transactions that they get in their best transactions. This happens in professional athletics all the time. A winning team, year after year, conditions the fans to expect excellence. When a team's season is even slightly less successful, heads begin to roll. Consumer empowerment has been driven to a great extent by conditioners. Conditioners are all around us, but for the purposes of the real estate industry, let's glance at examples from three industries—retailing, catalog sales, and hospitality.

Nordstrom's is the Rolls-Royce of retailing; the pinnacle of variety, service, and customer care. It isn't just the personal touch as a customer enters the door, but the careful attention to match customer needs with goods. Nordstrom's is the stuff of legend because it stands behind everything it sells, accepting returns with no questions asked. "The customer is always right" may sound like a sales pitch, but at Nordstrom's it's a way of doing business. The personal touch applied by Nordstrom's and its sales personnel more than makes up for the higher than usual prices. Conditioned by Nordstrom's approach, consumers are reluctant to accept anything less. The result has been the demise of many old-line, well-respected, but traditional, department stores.

Catalog sales is a booming industry, and Land's End and L.L. Bean long have set a standard for customer service that's earned them the highest marks in the business. Call either one and the customer service representative has your full history at hand the moment you're connected. The person answering the phone is knowledgeable and can talk intelligently about not only the product you seek, but also any other specials that might fit with your prior purchase profile. By using your profile as a guide in the conversation, the representative is able to generate real value for the consumer. This value added is available while you sit in an easy chair and, of course, any purchase is completely guaranteed.

There's a terrific advertisement for Motel 6 (which caters to the bare-bones traveler), narrated by Tom Bodett. In that twangy voice Bodett says, "When you turn the lights off, they're all the same." Well, Tom my boy, it just isn't so. If you're a frequent guest at a Ritz-Carlton hotel, you've experienced how customer profiling generates real value for their guests. Any Ritz-Carlton fits into the category of "fine hotels." Rooms aren't cheap, but they may in fact generate more consumer value than a Motel 6.

The Ritz-Carlton keeps a running profile of any frequent guest by using technology. When you walk into a Ritz-Carlton you'll be greeted personally. Your room is set up to your specifications. The hotel staff will know your tastes and your usual schedule. When you talk to a staff member at any level, you are acutely aware of personal attention. When you dial room service, your consuming profile with the Ritz-Carlton is on a computer screen before the phone is answered. Any particular taste (ice in your wine, meat cooked well-done) is noted and accommodated with your order. In short, the Ritz-Carlton is setting a level of service that the consumer will expect in any fine hotel.

It isn't only the upper end of the hotel spectrum that is catering to the customer's tastes. The "suite" concept, increasingly with business services provided in the room, has grown dramatically. For the frequent business traveler, these hotels are providing an environment that creates the feeling of being at home with the convenience of being able to work in the room. Rooms often have a fireplace, and the guest receives a complimentary newspaper, a free breakfast, and often a cocktail hour at no charge. Perhaps it's a stretch to say that hotel chains of this kind pamper customers, but they're moving steadily in that direction by helping to remove the drudge from traveling. And they are setting another standard for the consumer—space and amenities away from home and the office.

Conditioners affect the real estate business directly. Real estate is a service business, and consumers see it in the same light as hotels; as sales establishments, real estate offices are seen by consumers in the same light as department stores. To the extent that consumers have come to expect fast, accurate, personalized service from any of these establishments, they will expect it from the real estate professional. Competition in real estate is coming from the Nordstrom's and Ritz-Carlton's of the world as much as it is coming from the real estate firm across the street. These companies are educating your customers, and you will feel the impact.

Extenders

The second category of "raise the bar competitors" is *extenders,* those who are providing new levels of consolidated offerings.

At one time in the United States (and to this day in some parts of Europe) we shopped at specialty stores, going from the greengrocer to the meat market to the dairy store, and so forth. Now, we don't go to the greengrocer and the butcher and the pharmacy separately. Rather, we go to the mega-supermarket, the one-stop shop where everything is available. Remember the "codevelopment outlet" where John the REAL-TOR® filled his tank with gas, checked out the news on the CRT at the gas pump, ate a snack, dropped off his dry cleaning, and picked up some sundries to boot? These we call "extenders" because they essentially extend the ability of the consumer to save time and to reap the benefits of convenience by going to a one-stop shop. Like conditioners, extenders create new challenges for the real estate business by providing consumers with new expectations, which real estate firms will have to meet.

Extenders are companies that currently have interactions with consumers that don't necessarily relate to the real estate business, but that could extend their services to be some part of the real estate business. In some cases, they may also be conditioners. Disney and Marriott are good examples. As a conditioner, Disney prides itself on the cleanliness of its facilities and service from its "cast members." Marriott is experimenting with a system that allows the customer to call room service and get a meal precisely on time, in peak eating condition. Perfection, each and every time, is the goal. Both Disney and Marriott own and operate planned unit developments, retirement villages, and managed care facilities. So, they are both *conditioners* of good service and *extenders* of different kinds of services to the consumer. There are other examples that fall a little closer to the real estate industry, including the following:

- **Financial Institutions.** Companies such as Merrill Lynch or American Express that consolidate investment and banking services could logically offer real estate transaction services as part of their financial services.
- **Tax Preparation Services.** Service providers such as H&R Block might well offer advice about mortgages and homebuying based on a consumer's personal tax profile.
- **Frequent Flyer Programs.** Today, American Express and Diners Club offer points with purchases that can be used for products and services that could fill a large book. Why not apply the same concept to buying a home, applying those points toward discounts on other services? Frequent flyer programs and airlines them-

selves are "captured time" media, where the consumer is an automatic and captive audience. So, on-board TV selections within aircraft or airport TV give a marketer a big opportunity to make a pitch. Increasingly sophisticated electronics might allow, for example, a passenger en route to Seattle the opportunity to view homes for sale there from the comfort (?) of an airline seat.

Extenders represent one-stop shops. They can consolidate a variety of consumer services in a single location, whether that's on board an airplane or at the local filling station. Because real estate is an information-driven business, any other information business represents a potential extender that challenges traditional real estate firms.

NEW ENTRANTS

Real estate has traditionally been a "mom and pop" industry. Even the largest independent firms, until recently, grew somewhat haphazardly, as a reflection of the founder-entrepreneur. Now, there's a new order, with the entrance into the industry of companies looking to exploit profit opportunities and achieve a high return on equity.

The change that's occurring in real estate is similar to what occurred in the electric utility industry over the past two decades. For years, electric utilities enjoyed exponential growth in electricity demand, and a regulatory system that pretty much guaranteed a return on investment. Their executives and managers were members of every civic and business club, and before the "energy crisis" years, utilities' offices were also stores that sold household appliances.

None of this applies today. There's been a significant consolidation among companies seeking to reap economies of scale, as well as to achieve a diversity of income streams. Now, regulation is giving way to enterprise, allowing consumers to choose utility providers to a greater or lesser extent depending on their state of residence. The point is this: The halcyon days of utilities operating like semi-governmental entities are over. Utilities are now equipping themselves to compete for the consumer's dollar. Today, profits and market share are no longer automatic. They must be earned.

As ownership changes, so, too, does management. To illustrate, look again at the electric utility. Years ago engineers dominated electric utilities, and to some extent they still do. However, utilities now have far more to deal with than supplying power to a growing population. They are challenged by environmental, legal, community, political, and social issues, to mention only a few. Utility managers need to be schooled on all these issues to be effective. Real estate is no different.

Similarly, the real estate industry is feeling the effects of a shift in its fundamental structure. The most significant aspect of this is the participation of new entrants in real estate. These new players are funded with shareholder money. This brings to the table the discipline of the marketplace and a required return on capital, concepts hitherto largely unknown in real estate. The result is that all the players in real estate are of necessity applying greater business discipline.

Public money means real discipline, and that discipline will require a more businesslike attitude on the part of the real estate industry. Public money comes with strings attached, and that includes managers altering the way they operate and approach the business. But real estate tends to draw its management from its sales force. Most of us grew up with an image of real estate professionals as laid-back and easygoing—sort of "with the flow" folks. Now, large corporate owners seek out professionals who share their discipline, a no-nonsense, bottom-line view of the world. This is true at the branch, regional, and executive levels.

The picture that emerges today is a sea change compared to what the industry used to look like. Although it's not a perfect fit, because management is more attuned to giant corporate structure and practice, today's residential business looks more like yesterday's commercial aggregations. There are a number of new entrants to the real estate process because it's an opportunity to make real money. Seems odd, doesn't it? Real estate was a sleepy market for several years. But let's remember, these are not ordinary times.

One attraction for these new entrants is that real estate can help create efficiencies. Through technology, these companies see the opportunity to make the real estate transaction move more smoothly and to create a different value proposition for the consumer. And in doing so, they want to capture profits. There's a fertile field here. If you look at the numbers for mid-1999, the total value of all houses sold was approximately $1 trillion. That's a big number. Brokerage fees from these sales amounted to about $60 billion (see Figure 2.2), and this ignores the ancillary income—mortgage origination fees, title insurance fees, appraisal fees, and settlement costs. So there's a great deal of money to be made. Capturing market share through a better value proposition offers real profitability.

Now divide new entrants into two classifications. The first is *investors*. Investors are generally established firms that see synergies between their existing business and real estate brokerage. They've entered the real estate brokerage business by purchasing companies to create synergies between the real

FIGURE 2.2   Total Sales/Total Value

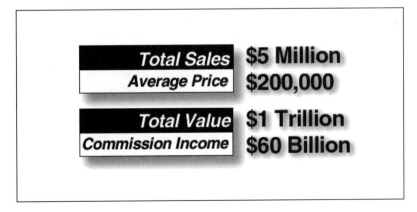

estate business and their current businesses. In sum, they want to capture economies of scale—looking to be involved in all aspects of the real estate transaction in its extended definition, and to use scale economies to increase profits.

The second classification is *innovators.* These are generally start-up companies that raise market capital largely through a venture capitalist or via IPOs, and use the capital to fund innovations in one part of the real estate transaction. These companies usually are in the mortgage, title, or connectivity areas—in whole or in part. But they're innovators. They want to make money by innovating in the market. Innovators tend to introduce efficiencies at specific points in the real estate transaction, and this is the key to their success.

Investors

Investors are companies that have looked at synergies, close or distant synergies, and decided to make substantial investments in the real estate business.

Cendant   The first and one of the most obvious is HFS, part of Cendant Corporation. HFS is a franchise owner, owning hotels and businesses in the hospitality arena. Over the past four years, HFS has bought Coldwell Banker, Century 21®, and ERA. They run them as independent brands, but the company has consolidated suppliers, mortgage companies, and relocation firms into a single large enterprise. In turn, the company uses its thousands and thousands of real estate offices as a distribution force to increase profitability for the franchisee as well as for HFS, the franchiser. HFS fundamentally used public money to fund these acquisitions and has been very successful in making the acquisitions pay off.

National Realty Trust   The second major investor is National Realty Trust (NRT). NRT is jointly funded by an investment community and Cendant. The organization has bought hundreds of real estate firms and offices. NRT is a "holding tank" for purchased organizations that will end up in one of the three brands owned by Cendant. NRT recently went public, providing it with public money to fund acquisitions.

General Motors Acceptance Corporation General Motors, through its consumer finance division, and more specifically through its General Motors Acceptance Corporation (GMAC) mortgage division, recently purchased the Better Homes and Gardens real estate franchise. Better Homes and Gardens is not a tier-one player, but it is deeply embedded in the real estate business. GMAC is looking to build a network and supply mortgage and financial services to consumers. It plans to use the huge buying power—or demand aggregation—of the GM "Family First" group. Millions of people are employed by the "Family First" group—a substantial number of whom are now affiliated with or previously were affiliated with GM. The anticipated synergy here is more apparent than that of Cendant, since all GMAC services fall in the financial arena. GMAC would like to become a full-service consumer financier, which would include mortgages for houses and other properties. It sees dual income streams: (1) the use of BH&G as a potential funneler of home transactions through its mortgage company, and (2) the capture of the business from the million-plus people who work for GM or their major suppliers.

Mid-America Power This energy supplier located in Iowa has purchased a number of real estate firms in the Plains states. With deregulation, energy companies like Mid-America see control of the customer at the point of the real estate transaction as the best way to capture market share for their product, power. The strategy is to leverage the real estate companies to get new energy customers when electricity is deregulated—in effect, extending the real estate transaction into customers' power needs when they move into a home.

Insignia A multifaceted commercial real estate and financial services company that recently entered the business with the purchase of Realty One, the largest residential firm in Cleveland and a large full-service firm in New York City,

Insignia hopes to leverage all its real estate operations and reap economies of scale in management.

Arvida   Similarly, Arvida, a land development company owned by St. Joe Paper in Florida, purchased Prudential Florida in order to round out its real estate offerings and to use this base to expand throughout the Southeastern United States.

All of these companies, regardless of their products and services, share a common goal: to reap economies of scale by being involved in as many parts of the real estate transaction as possible.

Innovators

The second type of new entrant to the marketplace is the *innovator.* Innovators are companies that specialize in one or two parts of the real estate transaction and attempt to change the way in which those processes are done. The idea is to squeeze all the efficiencies and all the profits out of a particular aspect of the real estate transaction and capture the resulting profits.

The largest single thrust in this area involves transactions management systems. These are software systems that automate the current processes by which real estate professionals hand carry hard-copy documents between and among the various players in the transaction. Large companies such as Microsoft and EDS and small companies such as Real Cafe are currently developing these systems in hopes of selling them in the real estate industry marketplace.

The second most significant area of innovator activity is in mortgages. E-loan and Quicken Mortgage were early entrants in this arena, but a host of competitors has arisen, including the interestingly named Ellie Mae, a company that sells software that allows real estate company-owned mortgage companies to have an electronic presence. All these efforts are aimed at capturing the ease with which mortgage origination can be done on the Web, thus saving the consumer time and effort and allowing the real estate professional to keep his or her customer close.

Figure 2.3 summarizes the four categories of new competitors in the real estate business: conditioners, extenders, investors, and innovators. It is interesting to note that Costco, the large household supply and grocery discounter, fits into all four categories. It has *conditioned* consumers to expect lower prices on bulk purchases, and *extended* the concept of the mega-store by including everything one could want under its roof. But it has also entered the real estate business. In conjunction with Amerinet, it offers discounts on both real estate commissions and mortgage origination fees. So, it is also an *investor* and an *innovator.*

SUMMARY

John and Mary are not unique in embracing technology in their lives. The convenience it provides more than outweighs the speed it adds to their otherwise busy lives. While their wired existence may put them far too much in touch with those with whom they do business, it allows them to live a home life that is closer to each other and to their children than might otherwise be possible. In other words, it lets them

FIGURE 2.3 Conditioners, Extenders, Investors, and Innovators

Conditioners	Extenders	Investors	Innovators
Marriott	Disney	Cendant	E-Loan
Ritz-Carlton	Merrill Lynch	NRT	Ellie Mae
Lands End	American Express	GMAC	Quicken Mortgage
		St. Joe Paper	Real Cafe
		Mid-America Power	
		Insignia	
		Arvida	

"have it all." The impacts that John and Mary feel are being felt throughout the economy and society.

These impacts are the result of forces that are shaping what is, in effect, a new economy. This is an economy in transition, one that is changing as profoundly as it did over a century ago when it moved from being agricultural-based to manufacturing-based. The social and political disruption it caused confused many people, but set the framework for most of the Twentieth Century. Today, the United States—indeed, the world—is shifting from a manufacturing economy to a knowledge economy. And the shifts in society and politics are no less severe. The environment around John and Mary is changing so rapidly that they are changing with it almost unconsciously.

Change is also affecting the real estate business. Part of that change is the result of those external changes in the economy as a whole that are affecting John and Mary's lives so dramatically. Some of the change is shared by the real estate business and other service providers. And parts of the change are completely unique to real estate.

The real estate industry used to be a cocoon of isolation. Real estate brokers and agents controlled information, and the buying and selling public had to come to them to do business. But real estate is changing, and there are four primary reasons why it's reacting to external pressures of all stripes.

1. Consumers are more empowered than they've ever been before.
2. The indirect effect of external competition. The entire spectrum of service providers with which consumers regularly deal are educating those consumers to expect higher levels of service from every quarter. Consumers expect faster, cheaper, and better.
3. There is new competition. New entrants are in the form of start-ups entrepreneurs. Well-established companies—in some cases, public corporations—are pumping money into the real estate business.
4. Finally, shifting roles within the real estate environ-

ment itself give rise to a host of questions: Who will be the transaction manager? Will it be the traditional real estate firm or the mortgage banking firm? Will it be the home inspector or the title company? The irony of this race is this: The Internet and information transferal allow *anyone* to be the transactions manager.

The real estate business is changing in dizzying ways, and understanding what has happened is less than half the battle. Throughout *Click & Close*, we'll explore ways to jump on the technology bandwagon and to *profit* from these changes. Armed with dedication, an open mind, and this book, you'll succeed in today's technology-driven business world.

CHAPTER 3

Understanding and Creating the Value Proposition

In the world of the empowered consumer, there is no brand loyalty. Access to information allows for a wide range of choices, and national advertising of brand names is offset by the hard facts available electronically. So, new and relatively obscure products—hitherto at a real disadvantage in the market—can compete directly and effectively with the names you read in the newspaper and see on television every day. *If you cannot bring to the consumer a real value proposition, one that offers an advantage and meets the consumer's needs, you will not succeed in the marketplace.* And this is true of goods *and* services.

So how do you do this? How do you go about positioning yourself in the market so that you can deliver real value to the consumer? This isn't rocket science. If you know why consumers place value on products and services, you'll know how to use this to your advantage and bring those consumers to you. This is a basic principle of human behavior and a key to good management.

Suppose you're given the job of motivating a group of people—at the office or even kids involved in Little League baseball. It's pretty clear that not everyone is motivated the same way. Some people respond to emotions, others do not. Some people, particularly creative people, need to have a great deal of space. Others need close supervision. Good managers understand how people with different personalities respond, and act accordingly. Poor managers are likely to assume that "one size fits all." It's really no different with your customers. While there are certain commonalities among consumers, essentially each consumer is looking for a specific set of rewards when entering a transaction.

What's the best way to determine what consumers' value? The best way is often the easiest and most straightforward: ASK THEM! In reality, the only people who know what consumers' value are consumers themselves. Until you understand that, you can't produce the value proposition or track and lock your customers in for life. Your business cannot succeed in the age of the empowered consumer without a significant investment in market research. This means getting close to your customers and trying to understand their needs first before trying to sell them your products and services.

This doesn't require any sophisticated market research project. If you have the resources, it would pay to engage the services of a professional firm that can give you a systematic reading of the wants, needs, and opinions of your customer base. The simpler way to do this is to spend a significant amount of time talking with your customers and prospective customers. (The best responses will come after the transaction, when the pressure is off and no money is on the line.)

Of course, if you really want to save money, just read the rest of this chapter. When you ask consumers what gives them value in the real estate market (or in any market for that matter), they'll probably tell you the same four major influences that make up the value proposition. They are:

1. Time
2. Stress
3. Convenience
4. Service

TIME

Let's return for a moment to the household of John and Mary Jackson, our two-income family on Quail Ridge Drive. Even with a load of technology at their beck and call, there isn't enough time in the day for them to handle all of their professional and domestic obligations. Workweeks are stretched even as salaries and benefits are good. People are prospering economically, but there appears to be a shortage of time. Many serious studies suggest that Americans have far less free time available than in the past, and that work, rather than home, has become the focus of their concern.

And the demands on what little free time there is are multiplied. In this hectic and seemingly more dangerous world, making sure children receive the attention they need and deserve is crucial. Helping and guiding our children on how to get along safely and successfully is important, given the chorus of voices pointing in opposite directions. This is particularly true in training and education. The job market today requires advanced technical skills and broad knowledge for success. The best opportunities will go to the best prepared.

For these and many other reasons, saving time is precious to people. So, giving the consumer time is an incredibly valuable gift; a gift that will tie the consumer in to you for a long time. Give the gift of time by creating a system that meets as many of the consumer's needs as possible.

How do you serve the value demand of the consuming public for time? The convenience outlet that offers a multitude of services—from gasoline to dry cleaning—is a good example of how the integration of services saves consumers time. The notion that all these services can be rolled into one may offend the Main Street America ideal of strolling from store to store and passing time with the shopkeepers, but that ideal is from a simpler time. Life now is time-constrained and the old ways are an expensive luxury.

Whether or not the consumer stops at the multiservice outlet depends entirely on its location. In other words, to be a convenience store, it has to be convenient! People aren't likely to drive across the street if it doesn't suit their schedules. This has led some oil marketers to buy outlets on both sides of the street, making sure they get customers going and coming.

Clearly, the multioffice strategy has been a staple of the real estate business, and the oil marketing strategy may ring true. But what matters is not how many outlets, but how many services are available in each outlet. The service station thrives because of the number of tasks that can be performed at a single location. The time saved has a real value for the consumer. But in real estate offices, regardless of how many, only a single service is available. For other transaction services, consumers must either take more time and go to other offices or pay dearly to have someone else (in this case the real estate professional) do it for them.

The way to save the consumer that valuable time is to create a one-stop shopping center for real estate *and all its related transaction functions.* This doesn't mean owning a mortgage company or a title company, or even having a tight relationship with one or both. (These practices are common in the real estate industry and have done little to change the way in which transactions are accomplished.) Rather, we mean here adopting a transactions management system that leverages technology to give the consumer an all-in-one, fast, timesaving experience. The purpose is to create value for the consumer by saving the consumer's valuable time. Later in this book, Chapters 7–9 lay out how this can be done.

STRESS

Along with the demands on time come the stresses that plague modern life. Driving on crowded highways, working under deadlines, trying to find the time to balance a home life—all these create emotional and physical problems that are too often the cause of long-term disability and death. In most public polls, selling or buying a home falls into the top five sources of stress. If you are the seller, you are not selling a property, but rather a storehouse of memories about family and friends. Along with it goes the worry that the "new people" will not understand what this house has meant to you and will not treasure it as you have and as it deserves to be treasured.

Buyers are not just buying a property, they are taking on a long-term, regular, and significant debt obligation that will exist for a long time regardless of their employment status or income. They are concerned that the value they receive is equal to the price they pay, and whether that value will rise over time. And for both buyers and sellers, the thought of having to move from one place to another, disrupting their households and generating cost, is a major concern. The fact that they must haggle with vendors and contract with new service providers at a new location is an additional source of stress.

You can create value for your customer by reducing the stress involved in the purchase and sale of a home. Where does this stress occur? At just about every point. The purchase of a home is an emotional decision. When the buyer sees that dream home, something clicks and all the rational guidelines coolly thought out ahead of time go by the boards. So a contract is offered and the stress builds:

- Will my bid be the winner (an important consideration in the hot markets of the late 1990s)?
- Will my mortgage application be approved?
- Will the home inspection results be satisfactory?
- Will the house appraise at the right price?

Most people are making the largest single purchase of their lives when buying a home, and that purchase process can take several months. During those months, as the process drags on, there are roadblocks everywhere. Our society has conditioned us to instant gratification, and has taught us to take direct and decisive steps to get satisfaction. Given this conditioning, buying or selling a home (and often one household is involved in both processes simultaneously) is like being in a mini torture chamber that destroys the pride and joy of owning a dream home. Consumer satisfaction is like the public's view toward a politician. People always want to know, "What have you done for me lately?"

So, what have you done for them lately? The standard industry practice for allaying stress revolves around the telephone. The real estate professional will make endless calls to the clients and the settlement service providers to inform them about the progress of the transaction. In some cases, e-mail has replaced the phone. As well as this might work, it places a great labor burden on all parties to the transaction. And still consumers have the time and stress problem of changing all the addresses that identify them to the U.S. Postal Service, the Board of Elections, the Motor Vehicle Bureau, the power companies, and even the garbage collectors.

The value proposition here requires you to do two things. First, you need to adopt an automatic and electronic system for connecting the client to the settlement service providers. Most transactions management systems now under development have such a feature, one that enables the consumer access to up-to-the-minute information on the status of the transaction.

The second thing you need to do is to extend your service inventory. The time and stress spent changing all the official documents that identify people by their addresses and the time and stress spent dealing with utilities can more easily be done through the real estate office. Creating these linkages within your business will generate significant value for the consumer. Later chapters of this book discuss this process further.

CONVENIENCE

At the end of the year, large shopping malls are very interesting places. In a rush to get holiday shopping done, consumers cruise around, looking for parking places close to the doors of their favorite store. In fact, they will even camp out close to the door in hopes of being able to tail a departing shopper and get that shopper's parking place. This routine is not confined to the holidays. Take the car dance that occurs every time you go to the local supermarket. The rush and aggression to get a parking space near the door are part of the scenery. Consumers define convenience in terms of the time it takes to get in and out of the store, and to shop for items inside. If consumers can find a place where they can accomplish several tasks at once, is easy to access and easy to navigate, they will revisit time and again. In marketing jargon it's called "bundled services." To the consumer it's called "inner peace."

Notice the key characteristics:

- *Easy to access.* The consumer can reach and enter the store quickly and easily.
- *Easy to navigate.* What is there can be found quickly and directly without having to decipher complicated directions.
- *Bundled services.* This one place will satisfy several goals.

When the consumer finds these things, he or she will have discovered a source of value. (It's interesting to note that electronic commerce has the first and third of these characteristics, and will truly take off when it achieves the second.)

In the real estate business, only the first characteristic— easy access—exists. While customers can find the real estate "store" easily enough, the navigation of real estate services is difficult at best. Without the guidance of the real estate licensee, full understanding of the product being offered—the real estate transaction—is impossible. Even with the help of the Internet, property information has been encoded so that little real information comes through to the prospective buyer or seller.

Nor is the real estate office a true one-stop shop. For years, real estate professionals have forged alliances with other settlement service providers, but have not sufficiently integrated them into the process. Regardless of who consumers use, they are still forced to visit a number of locations to achieve the end result—a completed transaction. Once a contract has been accepted, the customer is shunted between mortgage brokers and title companies and home inspectors and attorneys—not to mention REALTORS®—to the point where one-stop shopping seems a myth or, at best, a pipe dream.

The stops needed are many and the time required is great. Until true bundling of services becomes a reality in the real estate business, the experience that consumers have with the real estate transaction process will be less than satisfying. It will not carry enough value to attract customer loyalty.

But is this true, or merely speculation? In survey after survey, the vast majority of consumers—two-thirds to three-quarters—say that they would prefer to have a one-stop shopping experience in real estate, even at a higher cost. In reality, technology means that you can have a one-stop shopping experience even at a *lower* cost. Put those two together and it adds up to opportunity, because no such one-stop real estate choice currently exists. Create one and you'll put yourself leaps and bounds ahead of your competitors, and add value to consumers. The formula can be found in the latter part of this book.

SERVICE

The great success stories of the modern economy—and we don't mean the "dot coms" that are flooding the economy and creating instant billionaires—are built around tending religiously to the needs of the consumer. This book (and others) have told the stories of hospitality industry giants like Ritz-Carlton and Marriott who have built whole systems around being there for the customer, when the customer needs them, on the customer's terms. In industry, the

Baldridge Quality Awards have spurred firms to create better and better products and delivery systems.

With the empowerment of the consumer by technology, customer service is really the ultimate value proposition for business. With the variety of options available and the erosion of strong brand loyalty, every transaction must be earned from the start each and every time. And so, while product quality has improved dramatically in the American economy, it has been service to the customer that has made the truly heroic leaps.

Clearly, REALTORS® have always put a premium on customer service. It has taken many forms. At its most trivial, it's the constant flow of plants, cards, and calendars that remind past and potential customers that the real estate professional is there and ready to serve all the real estate needs of the consumer. In an active transaction, it can take the form of diligent follow-up to the settlement process by remaining in daily contact with all parties to the deal, both principals and service providers. This service is usually effective because it falls into the area where the customers' immediate needs—a completed transaction—are clearly known.

But today's customer service goes beyond promptness in returning calls and generally knowing the customer's needs. It goes to *continuing* service. What provisions do real estate professionals make to keep contact with their clients and provide them with valuable information and services between the times they're actively in the market?

The answer goes beyond sending out an annual calendar. There is a large volume of valuable and actionable information that the real estate agent could provide to consumers that would create value. Pointcast established its market niche by tailoring information flows to consumers and saving them the time it would take to assemble the whole bundle themselves. Similar information tailored to the consumer would associate the name of the real estate professional with value.

Consider this. If you could provide periodic e-mail updates on interest rates, refinancing potential, house appreciation, and sales activity information, as well as developments in the general economy, would this be valuable to your clients? The technology to do this exists and can be leveraged in allowing the provision of these data. Some real estate professionals do this now, to great effect, but do so in hard copy, transmitted via snail mail. Technology allows for the electronic assembly and transmission of more current data in greater volume at lower cost.

Where's the value to the real estate professional? The average customer engages a real estate firm every five to seven years. Given the turnover in the business and the attention span of the public, it's doubtful that customers will return to the same professional, regardless of how many calendars and azalea bushes they've received. But if that real estate professional's name is associated with a stream of interesting and valuable information, it will more likely be on the mind of consumers when they reenter the market. To the extent that you can provide that continuing service, you will create real value for both yourself and for your customers.

So to sum it up, here's the value proposition for consumers. It's very, very simple.

If you can give consumers back time, take away stress, and provide a one-stop shopping center that yields continuing and excellent customer service, you've created a value proposition for the consumer that transcends the current value created by the real estate business.

Now, this isn't reinventing the wheel here. Look around. Recall the examples given earlier in this book. The value proposition is at the heart of most corporate strategies. So it's not an option if you want to succeed; it's a requirement to keep in step with most of American business. It's a proposition that will be fundamental to the makeup of the real estate industry and a foundation for success.

Someone will get this combination right and will be wildly successful with today's customers. The competitors are many. Every settlement service firm is in position to create the value proposition for the public. Wild cards like Fannie Mae and Freddie Mac lurk in the background. Older and well-capitalized firms from related industries like financial services are poised to add real estate to their line of business. New technology-based firms that can offer the ease of electronic communication to the public are looking to enter the business.

Note that all these challengers are technology-driven. Using a high-tech system to deliver real estate information to a captive audience is an example of "raise the bar competition." As an example of how this works, Land's End has systems that enable it to capture, manage, and use data, and create the perception that a perfect stranger is a long-lost friend. Look around. Potential competitors are everywhere and anywhere.

*C*ASE STUDY

A Recent Home Purchase

A recent consumer experience.

Bob and his wife are relocating to John's (a REAL-TOR®) part of the state. After perusing available properties in the new location on the Internet, they make a trip to the new city and narrow their choice of neighborhoods in which they would like to live. Additional searching on the local MLS Internet site identifies potential properties for purchase in the selected neighborhoods. They contact John, a REALTOR® recommended by a friend who lives in the area, and schedule a time to view the properties selected from the Internet site.

Continued on page 46

John is very helpful and his knowledge of the local area narrows the number of previously selected properties for viewing while his access to the MLS database produces four additional candidates. The REALTOR® is very attentive during the next two long weekends—much driving and looking—and two offers later a purchase agreement is signed.

Upon execution of the purchase agreement, John faxes Bob a note acknowledging the signing of the agreement by the seller and provides a list of three possible mortgage loan sources and a recommended home inspection company. Two days later Bob calls John and asks if, being local, he can assist with initiating the home inspection. John does that, and Bob's next contact is from John two weeks later asking how the mortgage origination is proceeding—because the seller's agent had asked.

Bob has now been cast into the mortgage company world with little to no guidance and little knowledge of just what he should do next. Dealing long distance with unknown persons in the mortgage origination process is not the most rewarding experience Bob has ever had.

At this point Bob has no information on how his home purchase may be proceeding or what steps he now needs to take to accomplish the move. Any information he does have about the transaction during the last four weeks was obtained by making phone calls to John or to the potential mortgage originators. Bob is pretty much "on his own." No one is really in charge of the transaction. Eventually (hopefully), all will come together successfully.

Bob, the consumer, would have liked the following things to have happened:

- Better communication.
- REALTOR® correspondence by e-mail.
- Upon signing of the purchase agreement, REALTOR® provision of transitioning to, and/or interface with, providers and suppliers of needed follow-on services, such as the following:

  Mortgage

  Insurance

  Title insurance, escrow, and closing process information

  Pest control inspection

  Home inspection services

  Moving household goods

  Municipality information (i.e., garbage collection, street parking restrictions, etc.)

  Association covenants or restrictions (if not needed and provided prior to purchase)

  Utilities information and any prepayment requirements

- A single point of contact for all transaction-related services.
- An Internet "transaction status site," provided by that single point of contact, where the consumer could review, real-time if you will, the progress status of the transaction components.

CHAPTER 4

Creating a Strategic Plan

It's often been said that if you do not plan for the future you do not have one. That has never been truer than it is now. The reasons are essentially two-fold. First, change and uncertainty have never before been as intense in the real estate business. This means that thinking about the future and trying to position your business to take advantage of opportunities and ward off threats is crucial to survival. In a world where technology has transformed the way that information is treated and communicated, and in a business where new competitors are rife, managing through change requires not only a plan, but also a *strategic approach* to the future.

Second, it is impossible to run a business in any environment without a clear vision of the future. Microsoft asks, "Where do you want to go today?"; the world demands, "Where do you want to go in your future?" When Alice encountered the Cheshire Cat at a fork in the road, she inquired about which fork to take. The cat asked her where she was headed, and she replied she didn't know. "Well," the cat answered, "then either fork will get you there." The point is that a clear sense of direction is crucial to the achievement of goals.

All of this is probably very familiar. But how do you go about creating a strategic plan that will prepare you for the future without spending a bunch a bucks to hire some over-paid consultant? The answer is in this chapter, which gives a step-by-step approach to planning that will get you where you need to be with as little outside help as possible. Some of this chapter may be too theoretical for your taste, so pick and choose. The point is to stay focused far enough in the future so that the business strategy you create will drive you toward your ultimate goals. Why have a chapter on strategic planning in a book on how technology is forcing a new business model? Because you can't get there from here without a good road map.

ESTABLISH YOUR VISION

The cardinal rule of a sound strategic plan is start in the future and then deal with the present. In other words, look forward by looking backward. The first task is to establish a vision for the long-term future. Where do you want to be in ten or twenty years? The answer here is not a vague notion like "rich and famous" that applies to everybody. Instead, you need to create a vision for the future in as specific terms as possible. The vision is designed for internal consumption. It is meant to keep you and your colleagues focused on the things necessary to drive the business toward its ultimate goal on a day-to-day basis. The vision should be clear and compelling, sufficient to motivate actions that will generate benefits for you and your business.

Core Ideology

The vision begins with knowing who you are. Every individual, every firm lives according to a *core ideology*. It gets to the very heart of the individual and the business. This ideology specifies why you exist and how you operate.

Core Purpose   The first part of the core ideology is the *core purpose* of the business. The path to understanding core purpose begins with the simple question of why you are in business, and then proceeds through a series of inquiries until no other answer is possible. For the real estate firm, this may start with an answer such as, "to help people buy and sell real estate." You then keep asking yourself, "Why is that important?" until you run out of answers. That is your core purpose.

Figure 4.1 lists the core purpose of a number of prominent enterprises. Notice the one for the Disney Company: "To make people happy." The people of Disney live this purpose. If you want to be given extremely personal service at a Disney property, simply mention to one of the cast members (not employees) that you're not happy. They will bend over back-

FIGURE 4.1   Core Purpose Examples

Core Purpose Examples

3M - To solve unsolved problems innovatively.

Fannie Mae - To strengthen the social fabric by continually democratizing home ownership.

Israel - To provide a secure home on Earth for the Jewish people.

Merck - To preserve and improve human life.

Wal-Mart - To give ordinary folks the chance to buy the same things as rich people.

Walt Disney - To make people happy.

ward to make you happy. Note that core purpose is an overriding ideal that never changes. Disney's posture in the marketplace has changed over time, from animation shop to movie and TV producer to developer and operator of theme parks to cruise line. Yet all these activities are consistent with its single core purpose. While its manifestation in the marketplace may change, a company's *core purpose should never change.*

Core Values   The second part of the core ideology, *core values,* describes how you operate. These values provide a framework for action; determine how you treat your colleagues, competitors, and customers; and show the external world your character. Everyone and every enterprise has core values. Ironically, *values* is a value-free word. Churches have values, but so do tyrannies; saints have values, but so do serial killers. For most of us, however, values are often unconscious and unexpressed. Declaring that you have certain values does not give you that profile. Rather, values are expressed only through actions. What people do and what they reward reveals more about what they treasure than what is said. Remember, assimilating values you do not now possess is an extremely difficult and time-consuming process. It is better to begin by analyzing your current values and then integrating them into your vision.

Envisioned Future

The next part of the vision is your *envisioned future,* or the world you expect to inhabit in the future as a result of your actions.

Big, Hairy, Audacious Goal (BHAG)   The first part of your envisioned future is your *big, hairy, audacious goal.* The easiest way to categorize this is as "what you want to be when you grow up." In the current context, this means where you want your business to be twenty years from now. What is it?

Thirty percent market share in your area? Creating a full-service firm? The goal should be sufficiently out of reach that it's possible but not probable. Think about the answers children give when you ask them what they want to be when they grow up. The chances that they will actually achieve their goal are minuscule—but achievement is possible. More importantly, taking the steps necessary to achieve a goal will have a positive impact on a child's life.

Vivid Description But specifying the BHAG is not enough. To truly reach for that goal with passion, you need to be able to sense it, feel it, and most of all believe in yourself to achieve the vision. That requires that the goal be accompanied by a *vivid description*. You need to capture, in as much detail as possible, what success in achieving the vision will feel like, how your business will be perceived, and the reward that will flow through to you and your partners on the journey.

These four elements—core purpose; core values; big, hairy, audacious goal; and vivid description (see Figure 4.2 on page 54 for definitions)—make up the vision for your business. Once a vision is in place, it's time to take the steps needed to get you there. It's like the Cheshire Cat said to Alice: It depends on where you want to go. In other words, you need to bridge the gap between current reality and the envisioned future.

PLAN TO REALIZE YOUR VISION

Once the vision is set, planning consists of four basic steps: (1) understanding current reality and the probable future; (2) comparing the present and the likely future to your desired future; (3) setting goals and strategies; and (4) preparing an operating plan.

FIGURE 4.2 Vision Definitions

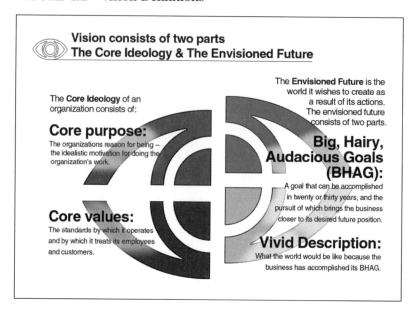

Step One: Understand Current Reality and the Probable Future

Begin by sorting through the relevant conditions that affect you and make some projections about the most probable future. Because your life is affected in so many ways that are unrelated to your business, be sure you include only "relevant" conditions. The way to get there is by using an *environmental scan*. The scan enables you to look at all the relevant factors in the world around you that will affect your business. In the real estate industry, these factors generally group themselves into five areas:

1. **The Economy and Society.** Questions such as where the economy may be going immediately and over the next five to ten years, as well as how society will operate, will affect both the demand for and supply of real property and thus your business.

2. **Demographics.** Real estate can never be unlinked from people trends. The trading-up process among Baby Boomers is driving the current market. The aging of America and the phenomenon of immigration will drive the future housing market. Finding out as much as you can about demographic trends will help you understand the future facing your business.

3. **Legislation and Regulation.** The political environment and the public policy positions of legislative and regulatory bodies will determine the way in which real property can be used and transferred. Projecting the future of legislation will help you plan for the areas in which your business will thrive and those in which it will be restricted.

4. **Real Estate Business Changes.** Currently, there is a wave of consolidation in the business and the power of technology is transforming the business. How this is affecting you and where it is going will help you shape your business strategy.

5. **Technology.** What is the current "state of the art" in real estate business tools? What will be the state of the art in the future?

The key to all of this is to keep it local. When you seek to understand the present and forecast the future, you must be careful to keep two things in mind. First, while global and national trends affect us all, local conditions will drive your business. Thus, a national downturn in growth matters little in boom areas where growth is still vigorous. So, when you ask questions about the present and future, pose them in the context of the market area in which you operate. The useful questions sound like this:

- What are the demographics of *your marketplace* now—homeowners versus renters, age distribution, racial and ethnic distribution, household structures— whatever is relevant in the demographic area.

- What are the relevant economics? Are you living in a boom area, a growth area? Will *your area* continue to expand over the next five years? Or, is the economy going downhill?
- What about the *national* picture? No one can be certain, but there are powerful indicators showing where the national economy is headed and what sectors are likely to be the most promising. These include inflation, interest rates, political stability, and regulations that affect land use.
- In business, what is *your* competitive position? How do *you* stand compared to your competition—in market share, in numbers of offices? What is your personal standing in the community compared to your competitors?
- How do *your* technological tools measure up?

All this is a tall order, big enough that unless your firm is large, help from other sources will be needed. Local colleges and universities usually are an excellent source of information. Professors are likely to serve as consultants for a reasonable price. The local power company is also an excellent place to discuss the local situation, current and future, since it must plan for the power needs of the community well in advance. Power suppliers generally have a number of programs to help small businesses. The point is, a third party needs to be involved in your environmental scan. Otherwise, you will be operating in an environment that is opinion rich and information poor and your pet assumptions and perceptions will blind you to reality.

Step Two: Compare the Present and the Likely Future to Your Desired Future

Now that you have a picture of current reality and a feeling for where you think things are headed in the future, you can compare these to the desired future expressed in your vision. Clearly, there are differences. Compared to where you want to be, the probable future contains both threats (things that are likely to happen that conflict with your vision) and opportunities (things that are likely to happen that will further your vision). Both of these present challenges. Addressing those challenges constitutes the second stage of the planning process.

In this second stage, identify the significant challenges that lie between you and your desired future. Because some of these challenges are already here, and some of them are going to arise as time goes by, you also need to identify the order in which you need to address the challenges.

Think of yourself as being in Philadelphia in 1840. You have conceived a vision that you will be a successful rancher in California. So you assess the current reality. You may have only a vague idea of where California is, and only scant knowledge of ranching. You may have a family that is quite content in Philadelphia and wants very much to stay there, thinking that your dream is a scatterbrained scheme. So your first challenges are to learn as much as you can about California and ranching and to convince your family to come along for the ride. You know that there will be other challenges—capital, guides, weather, hostile natives—that you will need to overcome, but without successfully meeting these challenges, there will be no fulfillment of the vision.

Step Three: Set Your Goals and Strategies

It's virtually impossible to do everything necessary to complete a process at the same time. Nor should you. To get to California, it's wiser to learn the route, convince the family to go, and buy a wagon than it is to worry about fording rivers and crossing mountains. In fact, some of the challenges of any journey will be unknown at the beginning. Once you've identified the significant challenges facing your business, you can put them in the order in which they need to be faced: tackle this particular obstacle first, and this particular challenge second.

The ordering of those challenges is going to set out your strategic plan. And that's the third stage of your planning process.

Now pick a time period. Presumably, five years is a good time period but in this world, things happen a bit faster. So, make three years a target if you're more comfortable with that time frame. Plot a path over that time period that will allow you to successfully turn the actual future into the desired future. In other words, plan to meet the challenges that you have identified. The description of that path constitutes the strategic plan—basically, the goals, objectives, and strategies (see Figure 4.3 for definitions) that you will employ over the next three to five years to overcome the problems and challenges that you see ahead of you. It's really that simple. You're basically picking a goal, seeing what it takes to get from here

FIGURE 4.3   Building the Plan

Building the Plan

Goals:
Describe the outcomes the organization will achieve for its stakeholders (members, customers, the organization itself, etc.) Five-year timeframe reviews every year by the Board.

Objectives:
Describe what we want to have happen with an issue. What would constitute success in observable or measurable terms? Indicates a direction - increase, expand, decrease, reduce, consolidate, abandon, improve, distribute, enhance. Three-to-five year timeframe reviewed every year by the board.

Strategies:
Describe how the organization will commit its' resources to accomplishing the goal. Brings focus to operational allocation of resources. Indicates an activity - redesign, refine, identify, revise, develop, implement, create, establish. One-to-two year timeframe reviewed every year by the Board. Serves as a link for long-term planning to annual planning. Sets strategic priorities for committees, staff and all other work groups.

to there, and envisioning the obstacles and challenges that lie in your path so you can overcome them. And once you've described the path you're going to take to overcome them, you've got the strategic plan.

Step Four: Prepare an Operating Plan

The fourth part of the planning process is something with which you're very familiar and something that most firms do on a regular basis: a one-year operating plan. The one-year operating plan essentially asks the following questions:

- What do I do now that I've chosen a particular path?
- What do I have to do this year?
- What do I have to do over the next two years?

Your current operating plan probably specifies sales volume, numbers of units, acquisitions or planned growth, and so forth. It specifies responsibilities, sequence of events across the year, and budget. When you have a strategic plan, however, there is one major difference: the strategic plan drives operations. The operating plan is the one-year manifestation of the path that will take you to your ultimate vision.

A great deal of this is malleable; it can be changed. If you find after a year that some of the things that you've chosen to do over a five-year period are unnecessary, or that new obstacles presented themselves, then clearly you must readjust your path and readjust your operating plan. But if you have a vision for the future, then what you are in the business of creating is a sustainable, competitive advantage for that period of time over which you are looking to reach your objective. Whether that's five years, ten years, or twenty years, you've created a sustainable, competitive objective. When you implement the plan—the strategic plan—through your operating plans, then you will have that edge. Stay with it and use it.

MEASURE YOUR PROGRESS

There's one final and very important thought here. Suppose you prepare for California, set out with your wagon and possessions, and after a year discover you're in Boston. Something obviously went wrong, and you've waited too long to notice it. *You've got to be able to measure your progress.* After six months or a year you must be able to determine whether you've reached the particular objectives you've set for your business. Any plan worth its salt has mechanisms in place to measure progress. If not, the plan is useless. Staying on target involves not only keeping the vision very clear in your mind, it also requires procedures for monitoring your steps. So within your organization, you need to implement systems—administrative systems, control systems, accounting systems—that will enable you to get a handle on how far you've come in fulfilling the plans that you've set for yourself.

CHAPTER 5

Thriving with Technology

INTRODUCTION

The management and use of technology may well be the most significant challenge facing the real estate industry in the next five years. This period will see reconfiguration of the industry on a grand scale, and the application and use of technology/data/information (generally referred to as Information Technology or IT) will determine the winners and losers in the reconstituted industry. Lester C. Thurow, in his article "Building Wealth" in the *Atlantic Monthly,* refers to our current market as beginning to experience a third industrial revolution, one in which knowledge is the focus and force. This chapter lays out a process to create a technology plan, one that will enable the implementation of the new business model.

If, in fact, real estate is beginning to experience a major market shift (and certainly many of us can attest to the signs), then you in the industry must prepare to be in the knowledge business. This knowledge-based business is a new model for many industries. REALTORS® must use the tools of the new market with skill and confidence. The platform for building new and sustainable value is not just technology and not just data and information; it's the combination of these *plus* the application of industry experience to create success.

It's not only real estate that is being prodded to change; it's all major industries. The Internet took even the experts by surprise. Bill Gates, in his recent book *Business @ the Speed of Thought,* admits that even he and Microsoft were caught somewhat off guard when the Internet explosion occurred. In a *Business Week* article, Jack Welch, legendary chairman of General Electric, indicated that he had to move forcefully and rapidly to ensure that GE was moving into the Internet space.[1] In that same *Business Week* article, many of the nation's traditional business leaders recount how they are moving their companies to address the new online marketplace. There is this familiar theme within the real estate industry: we are threatened; we must keep up; we must become "e-conscious."

THE ROLE OF TECHNOLOGY IN THE REAL ESTATE FIRM

The task is perhaps more daunting for those in real estate than it is for those in other industries because REALTORS® have not considered automation an integral part of their business. Further, because most of the participants in real estate are independent contractors, it is often difficult to mandate company-wide efficiencies. Companies in other industries simply mandate standard hardware and software, standard database structures, and centralized data files. Other industries gain operational efficiencies from automation that are not necessarily realized by real estate companies. Figure 5.1 describes the data used in the real estate transaction. This data is located

---

[1] In a recent conversation with Michele Weigand, VP of Business Development for GE Capital Mortgage, she indicated that a major push was on inside all of GE to embrace e-commerce.

FIGURE 5.1   Islands of Information

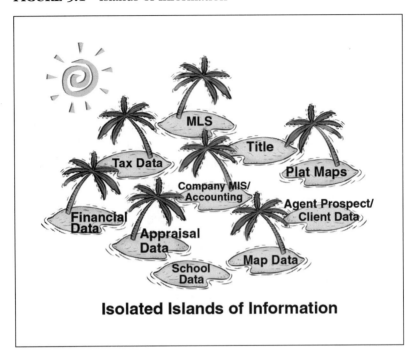

Isolated Islands of Information

on "islands," isolated and rarely integrated. Multiple Listing Data is not well-integrated with property data, school data, demographic data, map data, community data, and other information. Most of the data and automation within each of the millions of home sales transactions that occur every year is not integrated. Even simple work orders are often handled manually. We have grown up with these "islands of information," and in some cases we intentionally keep them isolated in order to protect one or more of the service vendors connected to a particular piece of the industry.

Unlike most other major industries, real estate does *not* have a technology plan. Many industries even have technology plans that support their business plan. This is a new concept for the real estate industry. Technology and automation generally have been viewed as cost centers that have little to do with the overall strategy of the real estate business—good and necessary, but not vital unless that month-end report doesn't show up on the CEO's desk. In the real estate industry, management information systems (MIS) deals with automated accounting and check writing, MLS systems, and automated MLS books. But, in most cases, even these simple systems are not connected and integrated. In some companies, an effort has been made to move beyond the automation hub of accounting and begin to capture data earlier in the transaction, and thus begin the task of predictive business modeling and projecting cash flow.[2]

In most real estate companies today, automation efforts fall short of full integration of data and information use. Even simple integration, such as having data on the listing form flow through a system to the completion of a transaction, is not often done. Instead, the same data is entered and reentered many times, sometimes by the same person at the same desk. Enter here, enter there, print it out, fax it here, and attempt to keep track of what has been done and what has not. At the Connect '99 Conference in California, Brad Inman mentioned that in a recent real estate transaction he counted 104 pieces of paper and the involvement of 43 people.

But there are many barriers to even the simplest automation within the real estate industry, where the involvement of many individuals, the different manual and automation systems in the different organizations involved in property transactions, the legal requirements for paper trails and recordation, and other types of information may be partially responsible. But even simple automation projects within a single real estate branch office are not routinely undertaken. Perhaps much of this inattention to efficiency can be attributed to the belief that real estate agent hours are free. Even if

---

[2] Systems from leading accounting vendors have made significant strides in capturing data at listing and contract time in order to build better financial models for real estate company management information. These systems offer more functionality than most companies are able or willing to use.

time within the industry is not valued as it should be, time and efficiency are very much valued by customers.

Automation projects within real estate businesses tend to be done on a "money available basis," and not viewed as mission critical. Lodged in the current real estate business belief system is a fundamental assumption that adding another branch office will create more value than will a project to make the current operation more efficient. But the real estate industry's continued investment in bricks and mortar should be viewed with a critical eye. The new competitors in the real estate business have virtually no investment in physical plant. They start with the idea that everything can be done with technology, and that empowered consumers will take on the total transaction responsibility. Most REALTORS® believe this is an improbability, but the *technical* infrastructure that is being built will make the real estate transaction process more efficient and will forever modify and change the way that business operates. Until consumers are willing to have the entire real estate transaction conducted online, there will be a need for a physical location to meet, greet, discuss, decide, sign, and settle. The strictly electronic vendors will quickly find that cyber delivery will not suffice, and they will need physical locations. It will be easier for these innovative companies to open locations than for the traditional real estate companies to adapt to a technologically-enabled transaction.

In most real estate companies, the producing agents use desktop systems, which often are not integrated with the broker systems. The most popular of these is Top Producer. Top Producer is not necessarily a barrier to integration; in fact, Top Producer provides export utility programs to facilitate the use of stored data in other applications. In many cases, there is no system to export to since enterprise-wide automation is rare. In some cases, where there are enterprise automation systems, there are data and system incompatibilities. In other cases, the tug of war over client ownership between agents and companies is the major stumbling block in the creation of a comprehensive client tracking and management system.

Agents believe the clients belong to them and feel that giving up this information to the company may mean the company will develop and exploit the relationship to the detriment of the agent. It's a vexing issue. Most businesses do not have this fundamental barrier to data sharing and client service.

THE BASIC STRUCTURE OF
TECHNOLOGY PLANNING

It is time for the real estate industry to take on the task of comprehensive technology planning. Further, it is essential that real estate companies view technology as strategic and vital to the survival and success of their enterprises. The technology plan must support the overall business or strategic plan (see Chapter 4) and should be an integral part of the budgeting and time-planning process. Information technology would likely account for significantly less than 10 percent of the company's overall expenses, but it will most likely affect 100 percent of the desired outcome.

Since IT is an integral and vital link in the operation and success of any real estate enterprise, it should be a significant participant and contributor to the strategic planning process. Most significantly, in this evolving new real estate business, technology can create competitive advantage for an enterprise. This is a significant change for IT. It began as a department that was traditionally thought of as cost only, and has become an area of strategic importance that creates market advantage. And it's a department on which successful execution of a strategic plan depends.

It's alarming that over 50 percent of all IT projects undertaken result in failure. They are either ill-conceived, poorly executed, out of step, or out of time with the company's needs. Many are abandoned in mid-stream and the dollars invested in them are lost. IT is viewed by many CEOs as a vast money hole in the corporation that they know they need, and know they don't know how to control. If IT is to be used to strategic advantage, it is essential that CEOs become conversant in IT. Failures in this important area are costly in dollars, but also, more importantly, in market advantage. Many CEOs, because of a lack of familiarity and comfort, just "hope those computer guys will get it done" and that "we can use whatever they are doing." Many organizations have IT reporting through the Chief Financial Officer because IT is thought of as more an accounting function than a strategic operation. This will no longer do.

In addition to the CEO becoming IT aware, businesses need to have a competent Chief Information Officer (CIO), sometimes known as a Senior Technologist. The CIO should be a member of the senior management team, should know in detail the company's operations and plans, and should "own" the success of the company along with all other senior managers. It's not unusual to have the technology department developing applications and making selections only to find later that a significant acquisition or merger is in the immediate future. Consequently the current project, as envisioned and developed by IT, will not expand to accommodate the growth. Keeping the CIO in the loop is most important. The CIO should be responsible for the creation and execution of the technology or IT plan. The CIO should be responsible for overseeing the company's database and technology efforts and for managing the inside or outside personnel involved in all IT tasks. It is also essential that the CIO keep up with rapid changes in the technology world as well as the significant trends in the real estate industry. The CIO should be a proactive member of the senior staff, bringing new and innovative ways in which IT can help the business to create strategic advantage and prosper.

CREATING THE TECHNOLOGY PLAN

Creation of a technology plan and linking it to overall corporate strategy is so important that major corporations and consultants have developed a discipline that addresses IT planning. EDS, for example, offers to assist companies with technology planning through a process they call Right Step, through which they assist clients in addressing the role of IT in serving their enterprise. PROXICOM, a fast-track Web development firm, prefers (and in some cases insists) to begin all relationships with a session to determine overall corporate goals and directions prior to addressing the actual development of applications for the client's Web strategy. Use of this process, called the Proxicom Process (see Figure 5.2), is further evidence that this firm believes in the planning process and in making sure that IT is closely associated with overall corporate strategy. For additional information on the Proxicom Process, please see Appendix A. Finally, one caveat: Remember that motion should not be confused with action. Get the plan done and get on with the implementation.

FIGURE 5.2   The Proxicom Process

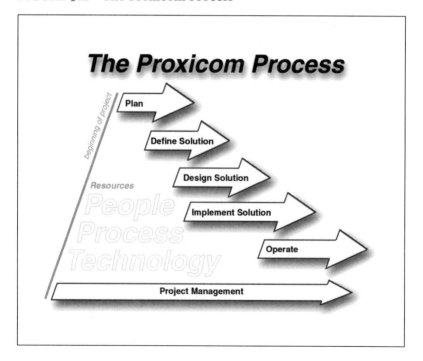

Generally, the technology plan flows as outlined below. The plan supports the company's goals and must, when completed and executed, create order and direction in the implementation of any and all IT projects.

SUMMARY STATEMENT OF THE GOALS AND ROLES OF TECHNOLOGY

This section of the plan should state the goals and roles of technology and answer the following questions:

- What do we expect technology to do to and for our business?
- How can we use technology to our advantage in the marketplace?
- How can IT provide employees, managers, and strategic partners with information?
- How will the company benefit from the application of technology and communications?
- Is the technology open and can it be easily modified and added to?
- Can the technology accommodate growth?

Figure 5.3 (see page 70) depicts the support that information technology provides to achieve business success.

PURPOSE OF THE TECHNOLOGY PLAN

The purpose of the plan is to set forth the action that the IT department will undertake in support of the mission of the business. Additionally, the plan needs to set standards for the procurement and implementation of technology within all the operating units of the business, as well as ensure, to the maximum extent possible, the compatibility of all IT projects and efforts.

FIGURE 5.3 Information Technology Support

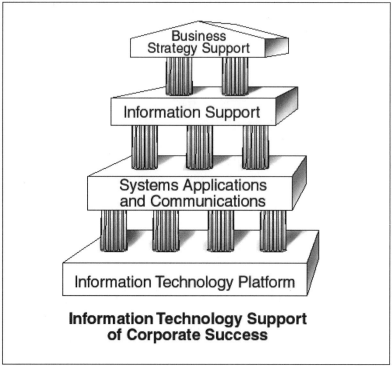

Business
Strategy Support

Information Support

Systems Applications
and Communications

Information Technology Platform

**Information Technology Support
of Corporate Success**

SCOPE OF THE TECHNOLOGY PLAN

The plan is to be the definitive documents that will serve to inform and guide the company in all automation undertakings and to measure the company's efforts in IT for the planing period.

IDENTIFICATION OF DEPARTMENTS WITHIN THE ENTERPRISE TO BE SERVED

As a logical extension to the scope of the plan, those functions within the organization that will be served and guided by the plan will be identified. All functions should be involved and instructed to comply, but there may be good and valid exceptions to this rule.

DESIRED INTEGRATION— INTERNAL AND EXTERNAL

Even though this seems quite obvious, territorial, contractual, and political realities may limit the amount of integration possible. Ideally, all aspects of the business should linked and automated links to organizations outside the company should be established.

ANALYSIS OF EACH ORGANIZATIONAL FUNCTION

To build an optimum technical infrastructure, all functions within the company should be surveyed and all functional needs understood and taken into consideration in the overall plan. In order to accomplish this task, an analysis of each department or function should be conducted. The following is a sample of what data should be collected and used in this process:

Define the Scope and Mission of Each Function

This task will not only define each organization within the company, but when all data are collected and analyzed, it will show areas of possible overlap or gaps within the enterprise.

Determine Automation Needs and Desires

It's often difficult to sort out the differences between needs and desires. It is incumbent upon the analyst to make the proper assessment as to what is essential and what is nice to have. If possible, collaborative prioritization should be undertaken to ensure ultimate users of the system agree on what is needed and when.

Establish Desired Timeline

Along with setting the desired time for project completion and for getting capabilities online, this section should clearly outline the interdependencies that these deliverables have on other operating departments. For example, if a new project in accounting has to be completed before the branch automation data can be used then accounting should have priority.

Address Expansion Requirements

What are the areas in which a given department could be expanded, and how likely is it that expansion will occur during this planning period? If expansions are likely, how will they affect IT requirements and what can and should be done within this plan?

Evaluate Existing Technology and Connectivity

In many cases, some level of IT structure or application already exists. Current technology and connectivity in place must be considered to ensure that any new planned implementation does not reduce the level of operational readiness of this business unit. Detailed mapping of data and information flow is most often necessary in this stage. Persons most familiar with the operation are likely to overlook important data paths or connectivity simply because of overfamiliarization. Detailed mapping of data and information flow will most often uncover the obvious but often overlooked requirements.

Prepare User Profiles

- What are the user profiles in this department?
- What are the capabilities of each person?

- How adaptable will each person be to change?
- How might each person react to a new system environment?
- How does the current level of automation challenge each person?
- What turnover rate might we expect if we introduce a new way of performing jobs?
- Are there leaders in this unit who will make any transition easier?

Assess Training Requirements

Hand in hand with the user profiles above, how much and what type of training might have to be provided for the desired application to become successfully adapted? Are training facilities, trainers, and training programs provided with the desired application or must training programs be developed?

SPECIFIC TECHNOLOGY AREAS
TO BE ADDRESSED

In addition to collecting and analyzing data for each function to be included, there are several fundamental areas in which decisions must be made and direction taken. These are discussed below.

Determine Overall Data Usage and Database Design

This is one of the most important areas of the plan. Selection of and standardization on a database engine will constrain or enable the use of data throughout the enterprise. This decision must be made based upon a number of criteria, as follows:

- How much data are we going to collect?
- What are the data requirements?

- How often will data be used and updated?
- Who will use the data?
- How will data be communicated or made available to users?
- What are the requirements to share the data?
- How will we keep disparate locations up to date?

Select Your Database Structure

Selection of the kind and type of database structure and the engine to be used quite naturally fall out of the proper definition above. Most often database size, complexity, and usage requirements are underestimated. Selection of a structure and product should always anticipate considerable growth over what has been requested.

Choose Your Technology Platform

The hardware and operating system you select constitute your technology platform. It is the basis upon which you will build the IT structure for the enterprise. This decision, along with the database selection, will form the key ingredients in your technology infrastructure. The most common mistake in this area is to be led by what is compatible with what is already in place and not by what is correct for the future of the business. The real estate industry is new to significant spending on IT, and may have unrealistic expectations about how much automation costs as well as its useful life.

Define Your MIS Applications— Corporate and Departmental

What MIS, accounting, branch automation, and marketing applications are needed? In general, what IT applications are needed throughout the company?

Establish Your System Throughput Capacity

What load must the system handle? How many users will there be, and how many sessions will they do? What is the level of task complexity? How much work must be done simultaneously? What is an acceptable system response time? The answers to these questions impact critical design criteria specifications. Information, once available, tends to create its own demand. It should be desirable to have the system used to its fullest. Adding capability as a result of legitimate demand is a *good* problem. If information is being used to further the company's goals, more use is better. However, if the system is hard to get into and slow to respond, users will become disenchanted and significant value will be eroded.

DEVISE AN IMPLEMENTATION AND INTEGRATION PLAN

How do you get the new systems in place without derailing the operation of the business? Implementation should be a coordinated effort, with all affected people well-versed on the process and informed about what is expected of them to make the undertaking a success. Users, system suppliers, software engineering, communications, power, contingency planning, optimum time to implement, and availability of key personnel all blend together to make any undertaking a success. Flawless execution should be the goal. Flawed implementations take a long time to get over. User and management confidence is shaken and hard to regain. Time spent in implementation and integration planning is never wasted.

ESTABLISH A TIMELINE AND MONITOR MILESTONES

Projecting time to complete the project and diligent monitoring of progress milestones are essential to the successful execution of a strategic corporate information technology plan. Automation projects are notorious for late deliveries, cost overruns, and user disappointment. It's not coincidental that these same projects are often the least understood by CEOs, and therefore the least monitored in any business operation. Nobody wants the bad news that another computer project has gone astray, and therefore few want to inquire for fear of getting just that bad news.

In his book *Business @ the Speed of Thought,* Bill Gates points out that some of the success at Microsoft is due to his insistence that he be given the bad news as early as somebody knows it. You can't deal with the bad news if you don't know about it. Monitoring of project milestones, and accurate and timely reporting, will go far to ensure the success of any automation undertaking.

IDENTIFY YOUR RESOURCE REQUIREMENTS

This task is to identify the needed resources both within the IT organization and in each of the organizations to be served. All the resources should be identified in detail and estimates on time and schedule should be included. Many times, resource issues dictate the reexamination of priorities and schedules. Conflicts can be resolved using outside resources, but this may require additional time and cost. The time-resource-cost equation ultimately must be resolved at the executive level, and all senior managers should be aware of and support the decisions.

FORMULATE A REALISTIC IT BUDGET

The final task in the technology plan is to formulate and present a detailed budget. Traditionally, IT has been viewed as a nonstrategic function and it has been relegated to lower priority in the funding food chain. If, as presented earlier in this chapter, IT is vital and strategic, then it must command a position in the dollar considerations commensurate with its importance. Underfunded projects rarely succeed. It is advisable to put off low-priority projects rather than to begin everything and finish nothing well.

In summary, IT should be viewed as strategic. IT can assist in compressing time to market for products and services and create significant market advantage for your business. Well-executed IT strategies go far in creating positioning for your enterprise in the new knowledge-based real estate business. Well-executed IT strategies are the product of technology planning.

Building the Right
Human Resource Base

Of all the resources necessary for the success of an organization, the human ones are the most challenging. Interviewing, selecting, recruiting, training, and retaining people are all part of the complex human resources (HR) mosaic. The challenge is double in companies with little or no HR staff and with even less expertise in hiring talent in today's highly competitive labor market. Since execution is the real challenge in all businesses (including real estate), ensuring that your company has the right talent is essential. Oftentimes it is necessary to update your thinking about the relative positions of employees and employers.

In the field of human resources, the current generation of business leaders has seen an almost 180-degree shift in company-employee relationships. When most senior managers began their careers, getting a "good job" was one of life's goals. This was followed by keeping a good job, which was followed by getting ahead in the organization, which hopefully culminated in a long-term relationship with an employer. Employers were generally thought of as having the upper hand, and keeping a job meant pleasing your manager and, ultimately, the company. If you did a good job and were able to stay on, a retirement plan was generally available to provide comfort in later years. "Good" companies did not lay off workers, and "good" employees could relax, having some degree of comfort that their jobs were secure.

That was then, and this is now. Now jobs go wanting for *lack of* available talent. Talented people make demands, and companies attempt to comply. It would seem at times that employers cannot do enough. The work environment must be pleasant, the benefits must be generous, work time must be flexible, and the workweek must not encroach too heavily on the rest of an employee's life. That's the new world.

Now imagine that all of these changes are magnified by explosive demand, and you have an accurate picture of the technical human resource environment. Significant salary increases, signing bonuses, and stock options are common-place in the recruiting of technical personnel, and employee retention is a major concern. Technology people may change jobs several times a year and instead of being looked at as "job hoppers" (an old term to be sure), they are seen as aggressive and in demand. Retention of employees has become task one at many company HR departments. At Ernst & Young, a com-pany so prestigious one would think it need not worry about retention, employee retention is a significant enough issue that they have formed an Office for Retention.[1]

In real estate firms, the technology HR challenge is further exacerbated by the fact that technology positions have been neither senior nor challenging. When IT is not viewed as part of the strategic advantage of the company, the managerial position in IT is typically thought of as a service-level task. It's staffed with someone who will tell the company which PC to

---

[1] In an article in the November 9, 1998, issue of *Fortune* titled "You Hired 'Em. But Can You Keep 'Em?," Shelly Branch estimates that the replace-ment cost for a departing employee can be as high as 150 percent of the lost person's annual salary.

buy and who can load all our favorite software packages if asked to. Many organizations seem to opt for one of two paths in the IT area. They either pick someone from within the group with a "leaning" toward computers or they hire a technician who has shown an ability to fix problems with the existing technology. Although these employees are often dedicated and willing, they frequently lack the vision and experience to help establish the strategic direction of the company and manage its IT undertakings.

If a real estate company does hire a capable IT professional, that person is rarely sufficiently challenged to stay long enough to be a significant contributor. Real estate companies are not fortresses of technology innovation. Fearing career and technical stagnation, the IT professional frequently departs. Another reason for their departure is because IT personnel are rarely included or asked to contribute at a senior level in the company, and thus they see no career path within the company. Finally, real estate companies are not traditionally staff-driven nor is the staff well-compensated relative to other industries. Even if you are willing to pay more to attract and keep talent, it may not be enough in this highly competitive IT labor market.

Satisfying this increasingly important need, in light of the opportunity available elsewhere for information workers, is a challenge. Your company is competing with every computer firm in the country for a very limited and very much-in-demand human resource. The situation is further complicated by a business environment that has not historically attracted IT talent. Real estate enterprises, therefore, are not a widely known or desirable destination for IT professionals.

There are two possible solutions to the problem. Your organization can recruit and hire talent, most probably overpaying because of the environment, or you can outsource the task using available industry consultative talent. Each has its own advantages and disadvantages.

ATTRACTING KEY TECHNOLOGY PERSONNEL

This course of action requires that the IT position's organizational level, scope of responsibilities, and compensation be clearly defined. Possible career-path advancement and job satisfaction are also factors that will impact the talent level attracted. As discussed in Chapter 5, the CIO or Senior Technologist should be a member of the company's senior management team. The scope of responsibilities should be comprised of strategic technology planning for the company, linking an understanding of the company's business plan to a comprehensive technology strategy, overseeing all IT activities, and controlling and ensuring adherence to the approved enterprise technology plan.

Assistance in determining compensation levels can be obtained from local area labor and wage studies or by consulting with a recruiter who specializes in placing IT professionals.[2] Recruiting firms routinely assist in bracketing compensation plans needed to recruit desired levels of IT professionals. Compensation must be viewed as a total package and not just salary and bonus. A competitive compensation package comprising for example, flextime, child/elder care, salary with bonus, and tax-advantaged retirement and educational programs, is the first important step in recruiting IT professionals.

---

[2] For example, Jim Adams is a Florida-based recruiter with national scope who specializes in placement of management and IT professionals in the real estate and mortgage businesses (jimadams@cmainc.com). He can provide an accurate compensation package requirement once the desired candidate's profile is fully defined. Additionally, most metropolitan areas have boutique firms such as Bollini & Associates, a Northern Virginia firm that specializes in recruiting and placement of IT professionals in the Washington, D.C., area (bollasso@aol.com).

USING OUTSIDE TALENT AS SENIOR CONTRIBUTORS

Having dedicated, on-site, immediately available talent is the most desirable situation. But often this is either cost prohibitive or unavailable. Outsourcing is a way to take advantage of top talent and only pay a fraction of a total compensation requirement. Whether candidates come from a firm such as EDS or Ernst & Young, or they are independent industry consultants, they have the potential to give great value at a modest overall cost. The challenges inherent in this scenario are that the IT professional is neither available on-site nor compensated full-time, and so your company has to compete with similar clients for the expertise and time of the resource. Building a long-term relationship with such a person or firm is desirable. As with employees, the task of starting over with a new consultant is costly both in dollars and time. One of the management challenges in this approach is that frequently "outsiders" are not immediately welcome and included as part of the senior management team. Additionally, "pay-as-you-go" consultant compensation plans often tend to limit the company's use of this team member. If your company plans to have an in-house technology capability, part-time management of full-time employees by a consultant rarely works.

Traditional compensation of an outside consultant is by the day, by the week, and sometimes by the month. This compensation concept falls short of the goal of having a senior IT person accountable along with the other members of the senior management team. Some form of contingency reward should be structured so that the outsource contributor has a portion of compensation tied to the success of the technology plan and the company. This novel approach requires creativity and commitment, but could have the proper elements of risk/reward. A form of retainer with up-side potential seems to be a workable model. Lastly, the relationship has to be long-term. The commitment has to be from both parties and must be balanced and fair. Like any good arrangement, this one should also comprise noncompete, confidentially, and termination provisions.

GETTING THE BEST OF BOTH WORLDS

A possible approach combines the employment of senior talent on a consultative basis at the senior management level with less senior but capable execution talent resident within the organization. If the technology plan is clear and explicit it can be executed by an in-house staff, and ownership of the results are therefore in-house. This approach may be the only viable one for midsize organizations that cannot attract, afford, or retain senior IT talent. It has the advantages of immediate and continuous senior contribution with lower costs and long-term professional growth opportunities for the in-house technology worker.

SELECTING THE RIGHT PERSON(S)

Of all the tasks that haunt senior management, one of the more daunting is the hiring of IT personnel. Most business leaders are comfortable hiring accounting and finance personnel. In addition, they feel comfortable hiring sales and marketing talent because chances are they came up through one of these functional areas and know what marketing and sales personnel must do and what skills they must have to get the job done. Hiring for a position in which you yourself would not feel comfortable is more difficult. Truth be known, while it may be uncomfortable, the process is not difficult. Some of the same processes that apply to hiring for other positions apply to hiring for IT worker positions. Defining the job, articulating expectations, and enumerating desired experience and skill sets are all necessary pieces of hiring for any position. In more familiar areas such as accounting, most of the details are known and understood and therefore rarely written down. In IT positions, detail is important and relevant experience and reference checks are necessary. The use of professional recruiters may be a worthwhile investment. Many times their probing for a job definition helps define the job and the right kind of person to fill it.

Technical talent and proficiency are not the only requirements. Fit with corporate style and culture is also very important. Real estate IT is not a well-defined area at present. IT is, and will be, in a state of flux for the foreseeable future. IT professionals tend to live in more defined worlds than that of the current real estate business. In the 1970s and 1980s, when people actually began to exit IBM for other positions, many companies eagerly recruited these fully trained computer professionals. Although these individuals brought knowledge and value, they were accustomed to a very formal and structured business environment, and style and culture clashes in their new environments were not uncommon. A cooperative and collaborative attitude coupled with business acumen is essential to smooth integration of the IT function into its newly recognized place of importance within the corporation. IT, for its part, has to begin to think about *how to,* instead of *why not.* The more global view of IT as a strategic contributor has to filter down from the top IT professional to all members of the IT team.

With increased reliance on IT as a strategic contributor within the real estate industry, it is imperative that IT make the effort to understand that business. IT has long been the on-call service station for data and technology. It is time IT became fully knowledgeable about corporate goals, operations, and finances. IT can only be the contributing strategic entity it should be if technologists venture fully into the business and take an active role in making technology work to its fullest potential for the enterprise. Toward this end, the IT professional selected to be part of your organization must possess the interest and ability to learn the business and to envision technology's role in accomplishing corporate goals.

7

Evolving to the
New Business

Businesses must be willing to destroy the old while it is still successful if they wish to build the new that will become successful. If they don't destroy themselves, others will destroy them.
>—Lester C. Thurow, "Building Wealth," *Atlantic Monthly,* June 1999

JOHN JACKSON AT WORK

It's Tuesday morning and John is attending the regular weekly sales meeting in his office, where agents get to present their new listings and ask the other sales agents if they have properties that might be suitable for their latest client. In addition to networking, which is a natural part of these meetings, there is normally a speaker or a training film as part of the program. This morning's special session is a film of a speaker at a NATIONAL ASSOCIATION OF REALTORS® Conference. The film is entitled *The Rapidly Changing Residential Real Estate Business.* The speaker is quite dynamic and believes fervently that there is significant change coming to the business. The message is clear, the presentation is logical, and the speaker seems knowledgeable.

However, in the discussion following the film most of the agents felt the message was too strong. Based upon their current experience, radical change is a long way off. Business is great and the more experienced agents cannot remember a better time. There are certainly no signs in their office that big changes are coming and that danger lurks just around the bend. There is, of course, the persistent rumor they are going to be replaced by the Internet, but they all know that's impossible.

John and his colleagues are right in many respects, but guilty of flawed thinking in several areas. Business is good today, and there is little evidence that big threats are about to empty bulging coffers quickly and permanently. Sellers are happy because their homes sell, and buyers are happy to be getting into homes with attractive financing. It seems like a recipe for continued prosperity. The flaw in that thinking is that it underestimates the ability of new entrants to perform the same functions with more involvement from the consumer, more function integration, and at significantly lower cost.

CHANGING THE RULES

Migrating a current business to a new business model is a significant undertaking. It is not a popular course of action, and it requires dedication and a belief in the need for the changes in direction and practice required by a new model. Even with the best intentions and a committed team, inertia keeps us doing things the way we have always done them. The re-engineering task is generally not assigned to one person and therefore must contend for senior management time that is occupied with the day-to-day running of the business. And, there are always a number of detractors who do not see the need to undertake change for the future when the present is so good. "Don't fix it if it's not broke," "don't tinker with success," and similar traditional thoughts creep in. Additionally, it is hard work to retool a business.

Many industries have undertaken major business renovation with mixed results. Continental Airlines, for example, was losing business to no-frills, low-cost Southwest Airlines. Southwest was a point-to-point carrier with no inline baggage problems, fast turnaround of equipment, no advance seating, and no meals. Continental attempted to create Continental Lite service that would imitate the Southwest model and allow them to compete with Southwest's pricing. They were unsuccessful. Not only were there problems inside Continental, but their passengers wanted the lower cost while expecting the same perks: advanced seating, meals, frequent flyer points, interline connections, and baggage checking. Continental's downfall was the impossibility of delivering no-frills airline service through a full-service company infrastructure. So Continental Lite had reduced fares, but with all of the overhead of a traditional full-service airline.

A more successful model is Metrojet, introduced by U.S. Airways. Trying to compete with lower-cost carriers, U.S. Airways built a separate company designed around a limited-service model within the company. Metrojet has a lower cost to deliver service and lower fares. In contrast to Continental's experience, it is a success.

The lesson is that businesses must be optimized to their service model. Delivery systems, customer service systems, technology systems—all business concept elements—must form an operationally cohesive, focused unit. Real estate companies are no exception to this rule. You could not, for example, operate a no-frills, reduced-commission business in the same location as a full-service brokerage. The customers would be confused, the management would be confused, and the agents would be confused. When, and with what clients, do you offer no-frills service, and when do the clients really need full service? Typically, what happens is that everybody gets full service and not everybody pays for it. This obviously is the worst of all operating scenarios for a business.

In re-engineering projects, having existing market share is a handicap. Building something new is easy compared to migrating to something new within an existing business. Business process re-engineering is a good deal like painting a moving train. The train is blue, and you want it to be red. The challenge is to paint the train red while it's still traveling down the track as a blue train. The further challenge is to ensure minimal disruption of the current business as it is being changed.

Successful re-engineering requires:

- an understanding of the current model;
- a clear vision of the desired results;
- an understanding of what is changing the market; and
- a plan to move the process from beginning to end.

Chapter 2 discussed the cause of changes in the market and Chapters 4–6 looked at the planning process. Now we will look at the current market and the desired results.

THE CURRENT MODEL

In order to achieve the desired changes and transformation, we must first know where we are and how we got here. Current business procedures had their origins in a period before automation or the advance of modern technology. Today, each piece of the real estate process or transaction is highly segmented. Each piece is also independent of the other. A mortgage company is like a machine that switches on once the contract is signed and the completed application is sent in. The title piece of the transaction has remained essentially unchanged and the title order is fulfilled through a series of independent reports and certifications. The escrow function (processor or settlement attorneys) awaits the assembly of all the necessary paperwork involved in the settlement. Each service is a mini-piece within the entire contract puzzle. The current model has remained the same, even as technology has raced forward.

We may use fax machines to send orders, we may even use e-mail to get messages back and forth, but each of these is still a manual process only made a little more efficient. True, real estate people don't lug as much paperwork as they once did. But many sale contracts and mortgage applications are still handwritten, or are handwritten and transcribed by typewriter or word processor to printed forms. The same is true for paper inspection reports, which are faxed or otherwise sent to the appropriate party. Often, settlement documents are sent by courier to settlement services or legal assistants, and the data for the settlement forms is entered by hand. Prior to settlement, clients are sent from hither to yon to get the mortgage, get the insurance, get the inspections, and so forth.

In summary, an old system has remained the same but made more efficient. But we still perform most of the process the way it was done years ago. The prevalent view of the current model is as a series of discrete and independent steps that end in an insulated, independent episode in the life of the REALTOR®, seller, and buyer.

So, what's driving us to the new model?

Earlier chapters in this book on how and why the real estate business is changing discussed the forces that are driving these changes. A quick review:

- Consumer demands and expectations
- Technology and communications
- Competition, both internal and external
- Economic pressure for more efficient and less costly transactions

Which of these forces is the more important is debatable, and pundits can even suggest additional driving forces. But there's no question that many forces are putting pressure on the industry to change, to be more modern and efficient, including the fact that consumers are becoming accustomed to higher levels of service from other industries. Consumers want the same attention given to saving their time, reducing their stress, and lowering their costs in the real estate sale/purchase experience as they enjoy in their dealings with most other major industries.

THE NEW MODEL—THE BEGINNING

Consumers are driving the new business models in most industries. Consumers get what they want. If consumers cannot get what they want from current market share holders, they get it from new entrants into the business who see apparent dysfunction as opportunity. So, a working definition of the new model begins with the simple (obvious) question: "What do consumers want and need?"

Consumers want more involvement in the real estate transaction process. They want a single point of contact to facilitate the entire transaction, handle all of the details, and keep them well informed with a minimum of interference and disruption of their lives. Further, they want to see the transaction as one continuous orchestrated event that produces a cost-effective and time-efficient process and result. This is the design point for the new model.

Most of us immediately think of the "one-stop shop" concept where consumers can get all needed services at one location—the Wal-Mart of real estate. This is the beginning of the new model, at least in concept. In its current incarnation, however, business in the new model doesn't necessarily need a physical location. The successful new model is an electronically-enabled center of all services that can connect either physically or virtually. Further, to satisfy consumer demands of being involved and informed, efficient management and tracking of the transaction from contract to close is the essential second part of the new model. Keeping the consumer informed will involve allowing clients to view progress of their real estate transaction online.

The SOMA Living Center in San Francisco, spawned by the Pacific Union Real Estate Company, is a good example of the assembly of information, services, and (yes) real estate sales and finance in one convenient central location. The Center serves only buyers. Consumers who visit the Center are not pressured into participating. They are welcome to "browse" the database of local properties for sale (both by REALTOR® and by owner) and become familiar with the neighborhoods and the greater San Francisco area. Further, once consumers are connected to the Center they can stay in touch via e-mail and search the database of available properties over the Internet. The one exception to the model of traditional one-stop shop is that consumers cannot list homes at the Center.

So this Center, this experiment, is the beginning combination of physical and virtual delivery of real estate services to consumers. It is successful, and it represents a new way of serving customers by a traditional real estate company. It should be noted that Pacific Union Real Estate Group, Ltd. did not attempt to open this new business within or colocated with an existing real estate branch office.[1]

SOMA is an experiment. It is a vision of the future seen through the eyes of the parent company's business leaders. It may not be the answer, but it is an attempt to try to find the next model or the next success profile.

*I*n a brief conversation with Karl Sopke, president of Pacific Union Real Estate Group, he was quite candid and open about the experimental nature of the SOMA Centers and quite willing to listen to any credible person's ideas about the Center or the changes coming in the business. He typifies the type of attitude that will be successful in any major industry restructuring.

---

[1] One note that the SOMA leadership adds to the mix is that their most successful salesperson came from Nordstrom's and not from the ranks of traditional real estate agents. This is not a criticism of the abilities of the current crop of real estate agents, but is more a statement of the service level, which is successful in the SOMA Living Centers.

Simply stated, the new model of the real estate business is about empowerment, service, and convenience to the consumers of real estate services. As summarized before, what consumers want, consumers get. A simple answer to the question of "so what will the new model do" would seem to be IT WILL EFFECTIVELY USE TECHNOLOGY TO GIVE THE CONSUMERS WHAT THEY WANT. Notice the statement is not "give the consumers what we want them to have" or "give the consumers what we can and keep our current revenue" or "give the consumers what they want a little bit at a time." It is GIVE THE CONSUMERS WHAT THEY WANT.

But the new model is more than that. It turns the old model on its head. Instead of looking at how to make real estate more like a business, it tries to integrate a real estate function into a customer service business. Chapter 3 looked at a new value proposition for the consumer. Chapter 8 will look at how to create a customer for life. Taken together, these form the heart of the new real estate business model.

Look again at the driving forces identified earlier, but this time with a twist. What if the driving forces are not only the consumers, but also the new vendor offerings educating the consumers about options or innovations on the old way of doing business? Many industry participants believe consumers are not driving the changes, and they could be correct to some degree. But in the final analysis, it doesn't matter who or what drives the consumer to want a new model. When they get there, the new model vendors will be the successors.

Inman News reported that a recent study of 2,355 respondents by NPD Online Research indicated that online realty sites are attracting 64 percent of the Web users looking for homes. This and other indicators portray a rising tide of consumer activity and consumer willingness to take charge of more of the real estate transaction. Web usage was up 50 percent in 1998, and almost 50 percent of all homes have a personal computer. Armed with knowledge of the real estate business and the undeniable movement of technology and communications (see Figure 7.1), the new model becomes apparent.

FIGURE 7.1 Technology Usage

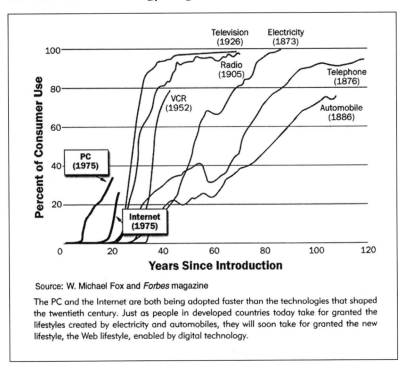

Source: W. Michael Fox and *Forbes* magazine

The PC and the Internet are both being adopted faster than the technologies that shaped the twentieth century. Just as people in developed countries today take for granted the lifestyles created by electricity and automobiles, they will soon take for granted the new lifestyle, the Web lifestyle, enabled by digital technology.

In this new enterprise model, there are four separate technology projects that need to be fully integrated in the business operation. While these technology projects are not all that needs to be done, they do form the framework for delivering the service defined above in the new business model. These projects are:

- Operating a first-class consumer Internet site
- Operating and presenting a one-stop-shop platform for services
- Implementing and operating a transaction management system
- Building a client-for-life value delivery system

Below are more detailed descriptions of these further building blocks for the Phase I New Model.

WORLD-CLASS WEB PRESENCE

Your Web presence is the portal through which online consumers see and judge your competency to assist them. It's as total an image of your company to the online user as your offices, conference rooms, duty desk, and agents are to traditional customers. It may well be the first impression many potential customers have of you and your company. Every sales training program ever conceived stresses the importance of first impressions. Over 50 percent of your customers will experience your Web presence either initially or during the process of working with your company. It is that important.

A world-class Internet site will serve the consumer throughout the client relationship life cycle. In the Internet vernacular, the site should be "sticky." Sticky sites hold visitors' interest for the longest possible time by providing content that is interesting as well as valuable. "Infotainment" is yet another of those words that describe many successful Web sites. In addition to listing information, the site must be content rich, providing real estate market data, current home ownership advice, and counsel about all aspects of real estate. The objective is to provide a site the consumer will want to go to whenever a shelter-related question comes up. In addition, you want the consumer to come back to the site between transactions for information and data about shelter and automatically think of you when it is time to sell or buy.

The site will have the following characteristics:

- **Ease of Use—Intuitive Navigation.** Today's surfing-savvy users are aware of the many options available when seeking real estate information. And although your site may contain the information desired, if the information is not easily located and presented in understandable formats, the user will seek alternative sites.
- **A Consistent and Error-Free User Experience.** If users encounter operating problems while visiting the

site or if navigation about the site is inconsistent or leads to navigational dead-ends that can only be backed out of, they will be reluctant to return.

- **All Listed Properties with Images.** Normally, the reason potential clients initially visit a real estate Web site is to look for properties listed for sale. If visitors perceive that your property database is lacking in any respect they will likely turn to other Web sources. Sufficient information about a property (text including address and images) should be available to provide a clear understanding of the property's amenities and whether the property has features that will lead users to want additional information. Many new technologies are available that create innovative 360-degree photo tours that have the added value of providing sizzle.
- **Efficient Search Capabilities.** The site search routines should accurately translate the users' desired home features into conforming homes and properties.
- **Interactive Marketing Features.** Interactive marketing starts with the collection of minimum information about the client: name, address, contact method (electronic or regular mail), and property desires (home type, location, neighborhood, demographics, etc.). As the client's property wishes are defined, an electronic dialog can be established wherein candidate homes, environment data (neighborhood, school, shopping, etc.), and financing information are exchanged.

As the initial "virtual" relationship develops, additional information will be collected into a database file creating the basic data for a "client-for-life" relationship. The client file will be perpetually maintained and enhanced with each client encounter. The resulting aggregation of data may be subsequently mined to determine when you might again be of service to the customer and to create a better and more value-filled client relationship.

Content

The Web site content should comprise any information that impacts the shelter equation, including the following:

- **Property Statistics** Neighborhood planning/zoning and demographics, and property value information.
- **Living Environment** Shopping, parks, bus transportation, freeway access, and so forth.
- **School Systems** Variety, quality, and breadth of education programs; school locations; and transportation.
- **Sports and Cultural Facilities** Golf courses, country clubs, swimming, tennis, entertainment, music, and theater.
- **Real Estate Financing** Mortgage information, loan calculators, lender data, and so forth.
- **Home Services Vendor Links** Information about, and links to, all types of home services and repairs.
- **Individual Office and Agent Pages** Office locations and services, agent biographies, and professional data.

ONE-STOP SHOP FOR REAL ESTATE SERVICES

Build, operate, and maintain a one-stop-shop capability to serve the customers of your real estate practice. This service or capability is designed to make available all of the services that facilitate the listing, sale, or refinancing of real property in a location convenient for the customer. These include necessary services such as mortgage, title, home inspections, insurance, and so forth. These services should be accessible by consumers or company professionals either manually or online. (An excellent example of the provision of such services is the SOMA Living Centers referenced earlier, which provides these services either in the Center or over the Internet.)

The provision of these services can be undertaken in stages. In the first stage, all necessary services should be made available in existing real estate offices either manually or technologically enabled. Offering these services online should be part of integration offered on the company Web site. The one-stop shop, even in its earliest versions, fundamentally assists clients in all phases of the transaction process—from listing or selling to closing—making it possible for clients to be serviced out of a single location and not forced into searching for all the various services needed to complete a transaction. The use of e-mail can facilitate communication to clients, as well as the provision of online links to lenders and insurance and title service providers to speed up those processes. While clients generally will be reluctant to navigate the whole process online, all effort should be made to provide access to those clients who choose to migrate toward online service.

The evolution of the one-stop shop could lead to stand-alone customer service centers either within the real estate office or (like the SOMA Centers) conveniently located in a storefront location and staffed with knowledgeable personnel. Display kiosks, computer terminals, and Internet-enabled connections provide consumers with the ability to browse neighborhoods, home types, and other living-environment information as well as perform definitive home searches. The home-search capability should provide search results with property descriptions, photographs, property location maps, and virtual home tours of selections.

Property sellers, as well as buyers, could perform comparable market analyses to determine the potential value of their homes. They could also:

- apply for a loan online and track the loan process on the Internet;
- register for e-mail, fax, or mail feedback of information;
- and establish a personal online Internet account for receipt of subsequent information distributions and to track future transaction status.

Finally, all data collected throughout the process should be stored for possible use in a transaction management system as well as cataloged into a client-for-life database.

TRANSACTION MANAGEMENT AUTOMATION

Every transaction is managed in some way. In most offices, transactions are managed in a rather disconnected "system" that is a combination of manual and automatic processes. Case tracking, as it is sometimes called, is the management of the functions and services that are necessary to move from a ratified contract to the closing of the transaction.

This process begs for automation. Manual tracking is cumbersome and error prone. With the widespread use of computers and the standardization of software and communications, the tools are now available to build a transaction management system and to have all parties to the transaction be electronically enabled and connected. A well-thought-out transaction management system will order the needed services, track the progress of each task, flag irregularities, and facilitate the smooth completion of the process resulting in a timely and efficient closing. Further, these systems should enable the consumers involved in the process to monitor the progress online through a standard Internet connection.

The challenge that still faces the real estate industry is the fragmented implementation of these "e-commerce" undertakings. The setting of different standards and operational methodologies will tend to slow the process and create less than desired final results. Electronic tracking and validation of the sales transaction ensures timely and accurate completion of each necessary task and streamlines the cumbersome paper process. In managing the process, the broker may enter the transaction revenue stream at contract time by initiating and controlling the needed ancillary activities. Through the transaction management system, the broker can electronically initiate the title process; order home inspection, termite, and other pest inspections; begin the loan origination application; and provide insurance contacts.

BUILDING A "CLIENT-FOR-LIFE" VALUE DELIVERY SYSTEM

The key to business success in this rapidly evolving real estate market is delivering value to customers. Continuing value—value that keeps the REALTOR® top of mind whenever clients think "shelter"—is the challenge. Chapter 8 takes up the client-for-life subject and suggests ways to build this value-based relationship.

THE NEW REAL ESTATE BUSINESS MODEL IS AN ENTERPRISE THAT:

- **Allows consumers to carry the transaction as far as they desire**
- **Provides online or personal assistance at any stage during the process**
- **Manages the process from listing to contract to closing**
- **Offers total ownership service**
- **Facilitates "client-for-life value relationships"**

It's all about making it effortless to do business with you and your firm, and a willingness to provide service and pricing offerings from almost nothing to everything.

CASE STUDY

An Inside View
By Stefan J.M. Swanepoel
President and CEO, Associates Group

You need a plan. A plan that will help you jump from the old paradigm curve to the new curve—the one with the "HomeEvent model" of the future, the seamless transaction, increased efficiencies, and higher rates of return.

Easy, it won't be.

As is always the case, there is not only one way of doing it right, but then again there are so many ways of doing it wrong. Here we detail a company, largely an "old paradigm" company, that in 1998 made the fundamental decision to re-engineer itself and become a "new paradigm HomeExperience" model.

The company, Coldwell Banker Associates Realty, San Diego, California, was formed some three years ago with the acquisition of a relatively medium-sized, independent, very localized, traditional, real estate brokerage. Insufficient revenue, poor cash flow, weak management, with one person putting out hundreds of daily brushfires. Pretty regular stuff for many real estate brokerages.

The company had one location, around 40 or so agents, and was at an annual GCI of $2.8 million.

Our vision for the company was to offer comprehensive, one-stop real estate services, consistently, completely, and with integrity.

The first step was to grow the company to critical mass as quickly as possible. Over a two-year period, six offices were acquired, the agent complement bolstered to around 300, and the GCI increased to $20 million. The company was now worth fixing and building.

We wanted to ensure that the company no longer looked or functioned like the amalgamation of many previous small brokerages, but truly functioned as one entity, one team.

That meant getting rid of all the many "president" titles, removing the confusion of multiple leadership levels, and creating only one place where the buck stops. The next step was to introduce meaningful resources by appointing qualified and dedicated middle management to take on the responsibility of executing the vision in areas such as technology and the Internet, finance, human resources, mergers and acquisitions, training, marketing, and public relations.

The second stage was to introduce a more corporate-like structure. Not a bureaucratic red tape, ivory tower structure, but one that understands the necessity to delegate, yet maintains accountability, with a structure that sets decentralized goals and timelines, yet assists centrally with knowledge and skill; a structure that favors strong individual project leadership, yet functions as a harmonious, integrated team.

Throughout the entire re-engineering process, all team members—the agents, the branch managers, the corporate managers, and the shareholders— needed to be in sync with the vision.

One of the most difficult hurdles to overcome was the need to achieve a high level of company uniformity and system standardization. To many who are not familiar with the industry, this sounds as if this might be a decision that dates back a couple of decades. Well, in many respects the real estate industry never

Continued on page 104

Continued from page 103
went through that development stage, and the smorgasbord of today is in dire need of sound principals of basic, good business.

We learned to challenge the traditional without forgetting about the basics. Do you have an employee manual? Are you complying with federal and state laws? Do you have company-wide policies or procedures that are documented? Is your organizational chart meaningful? Are the reporting lines appropriate? Do the managers have accountability? Do you have job descriptions and job flow, career planning, and succession planning? Have you implemented standardized flexible agent compensation plans? Are you managing your resources effectively? And so on.

Real estate agents are frequently hired for their superior communication and people skills. Brokers, in turn, are fairly unsophisticated about technology. Collectively, these two groups have been able to successfully resist technology for years.

However, if you, as a traditional paradigm player, wish to be around in the next five years, you need to understand that:

- The Internet has been transformed from a dull, slow platform, inhabited by techno-geeks to an exciting, multimedia, interactive medium, frequented by the "man on the street."
- More than 150 million people already use the Internet every day, 25 percent of all U.S. households already have an online service, and some $50 billion in business was conducted via the Internet in 1998.
- We will have ubiquitous, affordable, continuous, high-speed, permanent Internet access anywhere, anytime in most of our metropolitan areas within a year or two.

- The Internet is not a fad. It is real. It is the key driver and the very core foundation of the "new real estate paradigm."

How did we prepare for this? We started by upgrading all our hardware. We purchased new Pentium PCs, preferably the same brand, definitely similar configurations. Your future headaches will increase in direct proportion to the amount of different technology platforms and systems you are trying to support.

Next we took control of the software used on our PCs. We didn't use old, dated versions of software. Also, we stayed away from pirated software. We didn't waste time writing programs. And we were wary of proprietary and highly unique software.

Standardizing on Windows (NT, 2000, or '98) and Office 97 (MSWord, Excel, PowerPoint, and Outlook) made our lives much easier. If you feel you have an industry-specific need that Microsoft does not solve to your satisfaction, be sure that the product you acquire is completely compatible with Windows and can import and export data to and from Microsoft products.

The next step was to ensure everybody—from the top to the lowest paid employee—understood and used technology. Training will probably be one of your most difficult and time-consuming components.

We started by holding very basic Microsoft, Windows, Word, PowerPoint, e-mail, and Internet classes on an on-going basis. We started at a low level and built the knowledge of our team gradually up.

Then we decided which ISP (Internet Service Provider) could best serve our needs in the area, concluded a group agreement, installed high-speed digital lines (T1, DSL, or Cable) into our offices, and set all our agents up on e-mail. Speed, integration, and effective

Continued on page 106

Continued from page 105

communication is imperative. *A company of hundreds of people, all networked together, is the beginning of one effective team.*

We realized the services our company offers (residential brokerage, property administration, relocation, mortgage services, escrow, etc.) should have direct contact with the consumer. We designed and created a different Web site for each of the services and linked them all together.

With a technology platform in the company we are starting to implement contact management, MLS data processing, real property access, virtual tours, artificial intelligence form-filling software—even e-commerce and transaction management software.

We learned to do our homework. You should, too. See which software packages overlap, which fit your company vision, which are compatible with the platform you selected, and make sure they are integratable quickly and that they are scaleable. Go out and evaluate companies/products such as eloan.com, iproperty.com, improvenet.com, topproducer.com, mortgage.com, ameri-soft.com, realcafe.com, ipix.com, Bamboo.com, and elliemae.com.

Remember, the consumer wants the convenience and choice that large shopping malls and the Internet provides, and it is now time for real estate to step up to the plate.

The next step we considered was creating strategic alliances or joint ventures with those other closing service providers that we didn't offer. The options of cooperation via SA or JV unquestionably work and have significant financial savings. However, having all the services under one entity makes for easier integration, faster transaction time, reduced pricing, and better accountability. A strong consumer wins all around.

To that end, we decided to create a holding company that would own a controlling interest in those services we felt were required to give the consumer a seamless "one-stop home-event" experience. Over the last two years we have added two mortgage companies; three escrow companies; an insurance brokerage; a multilicensed maintenance company with plumbing, electrical, carpentry, and painting skills; a property management division; a commercial sales and leasing division; a third-party relocation company; and transaction services.

The Digital Nervous System

Currently in development is the company's "digital nervous system" that will serve the entire group, off the same system, accessible through the Internet.

Client and property data will be managed centrally, but its use will be decentralized. The data will be imported from existing sources such as DataQuick or Experian where applicable, and otherwise input will be once. Output, however, will be multiple—to the MLS, the national franchiser, the accounting system, the mortgage company, the escrow company, and so on. Of course, this introduces significant cost savings and quality data—something the industry has not been known for.

The Digital Nervous System will also endeavor to handle all internal functionalities of the company. It will be a place where a team member can go to see company policies, agent telephone numbers, commission schedules, job postings, updates on acquisitions, and so on.

Continued on page 108

Continued from page 107

Competition and the Future

Can traditional real estate companies compete with new technology models? Yes, we believe we are able to compete with just about any new paradigm "dot com" model the industry can throw at us, because we know our industry and we market inside out. We have accepted that commissions are going down, consumers are automated, and they want quicker 24 x 7 service.

And so we concur. It's coming fast—no problem. Total change—no problem. Many participants will leave—no problem. Some will stay. You bet—and we intend to be one of them. I hope you do, too.

8

Client for Life—
Not Just Till Settlement

Consider the activities associated with homeownership. From an activity perspective, customers view home buying, home financing, home maintenance, home repair, and home improvement to be logically related. . . . In the marketplace, however, homeowners must deal with real estate agents, banks, mortgage firms, newspapers, plumbers, electricians, lawn care services, maid services, home improvement stores, home modeling contractors, architects, and interior designers . . . to satisfy this set of related needs. In doing so, customers must search, evaluate and negotiate with a large number of service and product providers.

—Mohnabir Sawhney, "Making New Markets," *Business 2.0,* June 1999

INTRODUCTION

Does this sound familiar? You've rented a property to clients, only to run into them a few months later and learn they've bought a new home using another real estate company. Your internal dialogue then goes something like this: "Why didn't I get that sale? I worked like a dog for that $200 rental commission and someone else got the sale. I worked hard for my clients, why didn't they look me up when it was time to do another real estate transaction?" As Yogi Berra would say, "It's déjà vu all over again." Everyone reading this book has sold a house to a family only to discover that when the family was selling it, they listed it with someone else.

REALTORS® have helped move families from one state to another, and later found out those families bought a new home from someone else.

The reason for this déjà vu is pretty simple. Clients don't visit real estate offices with the frequency they visit supermarkets or hotels or even car dealers. They see their relationship with a real estate professional as episodic, beginning with the initial contact and ending at the settlement table. They do not see you as their REALTOR® for life—just their REALTOR® for this one transaction. You helped them with a rental, you listed their home, and you helped them find a home. For some reason, they weren't motivated to look you up the second time.

But the temporary nature of the relationship is only partly the fault of consumers. They have been conditioned to regard the real estate professional as serving only one function in their lives—the facilitation of shelter arrangements. So consumers look for nothing more. But fault can also be laid at the feet of the real estate professional, because nothing more is offered. This flies in the face of what's happening in the service sector of the economy generally. Most organizations are looking to create a customer for life by locking the consumer in to their services.

This chapter looks at how you can create a customer for life. In effect, this is the end result you will achieve by creating and implementing the strategic, technology, and human resource plans described in Chapters 5-7. By using these tools, and by managing information, you will develop customer loyalty that transcends the current transaction.

DEVELOPING A CUSTOMER FOR LIFE

Customer-for-life relationships are based upon continued visible value. In real estate this is a challenge because the customer does not buy or sell real estate all that often. When the customer only shows up every three years or more, the dilemma is: How do you deliver or maintain continued visible value when the *contact* between customer and service provider is so infrequent? The answer is: Shorten the interval between those contact episodes. That doesn't mean have clients list or sell more frequently (although that would be desirable) but it does mean that you should expand the reasons why the consumer has to deal with you. *You must be in the business of delivering something else in between the "big events."* Notes and postcards proclaiming "Just Listed," "Just Sold," "New Neighbor," "Happy Birthday House," and gifts of flowering plants and calendars won't get the job done. Most of those things end up in the junk pile for trashing. It takes something more.

Earlier chapters asked, "What do consumers want?" Now the question is, "What needs do consumers have that are related to their home, beyond the actual buy, sell, and rent transaction?" Real estate professionals are already associated with the home. It is only a short extension of that identity to include other functions and services beyond the actual transaction.

The opportunities fall into four major categories:

1. **Address-Related Documents** It's amazing how many things that identify people are related to where they live. And it's surprising how much time it takes to change all those identifiers when one moves. Mail is the most obvious of these, and the U.S. Postal Service makes it relatively easy to enter a change of address form. Of course, this change of address form is not related to similar forms that are used by the Motor Vehicle Bureau or the Election Board. Those forms are easy to use as well. Unfortunately, "easy" plus "easy" plus "easy" equals hard, in the sense of the time it takes to get, fill out, and submit each of these forms. The provision of this type of service, which is now being done by a number of real estate firms around the country, is one way to extend the relationship with the consumer beyond the settlement table.

2. **Essential Connections** More important than change of address are the real changes that accompany a move. Switching utilities, cable TV, and other essential services are, like the simple address changes noted above, very easy. But at the end of the Twentieth Century, all of these industries are being deregulated, so there are real choices for consumers at the point of moving. Now the issue for the consumer transcends the mere change of address; it includes weighing the relative costs of different suppliers. Increasingly, competition will radically alter the costs of energy to the consumer. The reliable guide to this new maze of prices will have the consumer's loyalty. The real estate professional is ideally positioned to capture that business.

3. **Home Improvements** The typical existing homebuyer will spend $8,000 to $20,000 in the first year of ownership, largely on improvements to the house and grounds. The list of possibilities for extended service here is seemingly endless. Painting, landscaping, repairs, additions, and so on, will all absorb a great deal of the homeowner's time and discretionary cash. Once again, the real estate professional is the reliable source for guidance on these purchases. Since the expense outlay occurs over a long period of time, there is more opportunity to get the customer's business—one more contact that can lead to a lifetime relationship.

4. **Lifetime Solutions** Most people exist in a multigenerational world. People are anxious to start their kids out in life on the right foot, and they look to comfort their parents as they age. The demographic profile of the United States today has sharpened these multigenerational ties. The Baby Boom generation is often forced to be parent to both its own kids and its parents. So, increasingly, housing decisions are made for more than one household over a lifetime. Setting

yourself up as the source of information about housing opportunities appropriate to the younger as well as the older generations, and advising families on the best way to maximize their housing wealth, is a function that can attract customers back to you many times—even when they are not buying or selling themselves.

*T*he "Metamediary"

In a technology-influenced society where individual actions can be broken down and analyzed, consumers increasingly see formerly discrete processes as bundles of services. At the beginning of this chapter is a quote that describes this process for the homeowner. Home ownership, traditionally viewed as a state of life, is in fact a collection of subtasks. But so, too, are getting married (scheduling, invitation, registry, honeymoon, etc.), childbirth (prenatal care, labor and delivery, feeding, child development, etc.) and a host of other personal and business activities.

In a time-constrained world, the old way doing these things—by seeking out and dealing with numerous vendors—simply doesn't work. That opens up a market opportunity for what Mohnabir Sawnhey (quoted at the beginning of this chapter) calls the "metamediary." Metamediaries are neutral third-parties who allow the consumer to reassemble the parts of the experience into a whole. By doing so, they create two kinds of value: they save the consumer time and stress (see Chapter 3) and they allow the experience to supercede the details.

Sawhney cites three conditions for the emergence of metamediaries:

- A broad set of related activities that are important in terms of consumer time and economic impact
- To perform these activities, customers should need to deal with a diverse set of product and service providers spanning a number of industries
- Significant involvement of consumer time and money

Metamediaries have always existed. General contractors, interior decorators, personal shoppers, and others have filled this role. But they have done so largely by expending manual effort. In the current economy, metamediaries are most likely to operate electronically. Peapod, the online grocery service, is an example of this. Another example is Edmund's, the auto-pricing service, that has now put together a package of services related to auto purchase and upkeep.

Real estate is a prime candidate for the emergence of a metamediary. The current process is too long and cumbersome to meet the needs of the modern consumer. Positioning yourself as a metamediary for the real estate industry is the path to creating the customer for life.   • • • • •

Each and every one of these opportunities is something a real estate professional can seize. Often, though, people in the real estate business define themselves too narrowly, and they fail to see where they can expand their business and develop customers for life. So, are you and your company listers and sellers or are you shelter experts?

CUSTOMER FOR LIFE AND THE NEW BUSINESS MODEL

In the new business model, the successful REALTOR® will be involved in the broad range of services that homeowners and their extended families need during the owning experience. This involvement is the vehicle for transforming the "customer until settlement" into the "customer for life."

But, many real estate professionals are already involved in many of these services. Coldwell Banker's "concierge service" and Better Homes and Gardens' "Family First" programs are high-profile versions of this. On a less visible scale, real estate firms all over the country are implementing some sort of extended service package. So how is this different from that "shelter expert" level of service?

The answer is twofold. First of all, it's that Web thing again. The extended provision of service for life will be best delivered electronically. With growing consumer awareness of the Web as a source of information and assistance, what is a more likely place to build your extended service presence? By establishing a private communications system with a spectrum of vendors, and then giving your customers private access to it, you save them time and stress in accomplishing the tasks surrounding shelter. Customers can go to a Web site, log in via a registered password, choose the service vendor they need and, with a single keystroke, access them directly. (This service can also be made available to those homeowners not yet online in the form of a periodic publication or a telephone hot line.)

The second characteristic of this new business model that is currently lacking is the efficient use of data. Chapter 5 discussed creating and implementing a technology plan to serve the enterprise; Chapter 9 will outline how to compile, manage, and use data. The bottom line is that, rather than allying with a random group of vendors, advertising, and hoping for the best from your customers, you use your knowledge of both the property and the owner to target market services.

Here's an example. You know the age of the roof on a house when it's purchased, and so you also know when it's time to remind the owner about repairing or replacing that roof. If you know the mortgage interest rate under which the house was financed, you can inform the owner when it may be advantageous to refinance. In both cases, you can present qualified customers to your vendor-partners, and you can provide timely service to your clients. That sure beats the broadcast advertising cards that are the staple of today's real estate practice. Additionally, if the consumer thinks of you as the place for information in between the "big events," you have a significant lead in being involved in those "big events."

INFORMATION TO KNOWLEDGE

You must use information to create knowledge. By using technology, consumers can do more and more of the real estate transaction by themselves. They have access to information that will enable this change. So, chances are, if you remain an information provider only, consumers will only engage you for the listing and selling of property. The key to creating a customer for life is to offer services that the consumer could only find at immense personal cost. That means you must migrate from being an information source to being a knowledge source.

You have untapped value. You know the area. You know the vendors. You know what should be done to housing and when it should be done to maintain and increase value. You know the owners and the size of the household. You know the size of the mortgage, the interest rate, the age of the property, and what will need to be repaired and/or replaced during the life of the building and the life of this ownership. Having all this information is by itself a gold mine. But when you combine it with similar data from public sources, you have knowledge—and consumers cannot replicate that.

These are important tools for building a value-intense and continuous relationship with the owners. Part of the modernization of your business model is the modernization of the value proposition you have with your customers. The key is using technology to manage data. We lay this out in Chapter 9.

A FINAL WORD

It may seem that there is no hurry to do this. After all, the market is hot, customers are streaming to your door, properties are attracting multiple offers, and life is good. But behind this short-term façade, the business is changing rapidly.

As noted in Chapter 2, there is a host of new entrants trying to change the value proposition in real estate by using technology to increase profits. The keenest competition for your customers is not from the real estate firm across the street or the agents you network with on a regular basis. It is from nontraditional competitors—companies outside the real estate industry. A new business model isn't going to keep those new competitors from entering the market. It's a way to create value, to allow you to compete successfully in a market that requires a close client relationship—one for life. It's a tool to span the gap between "big events" by linking yourself to your customers, utilizing a constant string of service contacts that yield value to the consumer.

Creating the new model requires a top-down business approach: design data structures, chart work and data flow, and implement open-system architecture to ensure flexibility. As exotic as these might sound, they will be as key to the real estate industry as traditional MLS systems were in the past. But unlike the MLS, the requirements of doing business will evolve quickly. One thing is for sure: Real estate professionals will change this program and structure on a regular basis as they use and improve it.

CHAPTER 9

Capturing, Managing, and Using Information for Profit

INTRODUCTION

Traditional real estate firms consider people who live outside their market area and have no current intention of moving in to be highly unlikely prospective clients. For the new model real estate firm, that's not necessarily true. It's not true because that new model REALTOR® will understand how the efficient and creative use of data can *create* customers. This chapter is about assembling and using data to extend your business and meet the needs of customers throughout the real estate market.

Consider this scenario: You sort a property record database for absentee owners, and order a current picture of the property. You load the data into the computer, match it to their name and address, and get their e-mail address from an e-mail directory. Now, you could be in a position to create clients out of these strangers by alerting the owners to the opportunities of a hot market. Further, if you send the information package (the property profile) to these owners, and you include data about current investor financing, calculate the equity in this property, provide updated value of their home, and ask if you could be of service, chances are they would be impressed. If along with this information, you include your e-mail address, your Web site address, and your photo and phone number, you've turned a stranger into a prospect and made an impression that might result in business. Both the information and the automation needed to make this scenario a reality are readily available.

REAL ESTATE INFORMATION

The real estate industry regularly collects a virtual gold mine of information. Information that marketing firms are willing to pay fortunes for regularly walks into the real estate office. And most real estate agents and brokers regularly throw this information away. Chapter 8 pointed out the value of an extended service profile to create the customer for life. The key to doing that is the efficient use of data.

Every real estate transaction yields four distinctly separate areas in which valuable data are made available. Buyers, sellers, transactions, and physical properties generate information that can be used to extract value. When these data are combined with database-mining software, modern communications, and Web access, it represents an opportunity to both serve consumers better and to increase the revenue potential in each transaction.

Real estate firms have stored data files that have enormous value, but most see the end of the transaction as the end of the value encounter and therefore see the end of the data's useful life. But each case folder contains data that:

- Identifies the sellers and their future address
- Names the buyers
- Contains the mortgage interest rate on the property and thus could be used to know when refinancing would be advantageous

- Could help to determine when the current owners might be ready to buy a larger or higher priced home or, conversely, to downsize
- Might indicate remodel cycles
- Could provide family size and age of occupants
- Might name the energy company selected by the owners
- Could identify termite and pest control company usage
- Could include e-mail addresses

And on and on.

TRACKING YOUR CUSTOMERS

Next to customer service, collecting data is the most important step a REALTOR® can take. Start collecting data the first time you meet a prospective client, and use every other encounter to do the same. Think about how many times the opportunity arises to collect additional information, including when potential clients:

- Visit your office or your company or mortgage Web sites
- Come to an open house
- Answer an ad
- Rent, list, or buy property
- List property with someone else
- Leave the area
- Come back to the area
- Refinance a mortgage

The list goes on.

Capturing information is essential in building your business and in delivering continuing value to your clients. Here's another scenario: Imagine a morning when you sit at the desk and review the morning report online. This report is an opportunity list that has been compiled from data collected and mined by the company's computer system. The opportunities are presented as follows:

- A list of renters who have leases within 90 days of expiring. With each name is a phone number, the name of a co-renter (if applicable), and one new and one resale home (in a moderate price range) that would be a logical move from this location.
- A reminder from a tickler file, which you created after each sale. It's your estimate when clients would be ready to move from a home you sold them, either to trade up, downsize, or relocate.
- A list of prospects that you have worked with who have just recently visited the company Web site and were looking at homes for sale. A quick click on the client name produces the last five homes they viewed on the Web site.
- Matches from your prospect list that appeared in the recent public record deed recordation report.
- Refinance queries on the company mortgage Web site are shared with the REALTORS® to determine if a move up would be considered before the refinancing.

Opportunities are presented on other morning reports throughout the company. For example, any just-listed property within the company is a prospect for the mortgage representatives, a possible relocation referral, a home inspection and warranty candidate, and a home services prospect.

MANAGING DATA

The management of data is critical to its utility. If data collected are to be used fully, they must be properly housed, maintained, and presented or made available. It would be folly to attempt to cover this subject comprehensively in the limited scope of this book, but it is important to consider some fundamental principles of data management (see Figure 9.1).

FIGURE 9.1   Fundamentals of Data Management

- Build the data plan to support the business
- Select the hardware and software required
- Publish the plan and enforce adherence
- Manage data centrally
- Make data available everywhere
- Keep the data updated
- Don't constantly change the data structure
- Allow for innovation in data use
- Plan major overhauls every 24 months

Since data and data usage are integral parts of the successful execution of any business plan, the data management plan anticipates future demand on both the use and expansion of the data structures and elements. Further, the data plan must anticipate the integration of data from all the company's business areas and plan for dramatic increases in demand for, access to, and manipulation of stored data. A technology plan needs to address the database software to be used and attempt to eliminate the isolated and uncoordinated building of proprietary databases within the enterprise. An overall goal should be to have consistent data structures, centralized storage of data, and management of database software and engines. An enterprise cannot extract maximum value from collected and stored data if the structures are dissimilar and access is difficult.

Each of us has probably had the unpleasant and wasteful experience of supplying the same data over and over within the same business or transaction. Data can be transferred and reused, and that begs the question of how wasteful and unco-ordinated a particular industry or business must be. This is the experience consumers have with our industry. Within many of our own companies, we enter and reenter the data for a transaction. In a study conducted several years ago by James F. Sherry & Associates, Inc. for Mt. Vernon Realty, we found that sometimes the same data might be entered 15 times within just the real estate company's part of the transaction. Similar challenges exist in many facets of other businesses within the industry. While you cannot fix the replication issues outside your company, you can standardize and coordinate within your own enterprise.

Creating standard formats and structures and selecting appropriate database software will go far to improve efficiency in the use of data throughout your company. The company technology plan (see Chapter 5) should address the standards for database structure, and establish software and hardware standards to be adhered to throughout the company.

Creation and enforcement of standards is but one aspect of central control of information. The purpose of centralizing information is not to aggregate power in the hands of the company officers. Rather, it is to assure that everyone who needs to will have access to all of the information available within the company. The second reason is financial. Compiling public data that supports in-house information is a task that is best done once for everyone. It's cheaper and more efficient that way.

Data must be easily transported and shared within the company for maximum efficiency, so your choice of software should be guided by its ability to both interface with the Web (in order to import external databases) and to be shared by everyone in the firm who needs information. Lotus Notes, for example, has both of these characteristics. Once this important step is taken, the efficient use of the data can be assured.

Keeping data fresh is a must. One of the major issues with the Internet aggregation services in real estate—such as

REALTOR.COM™, Home Advisor, and Cyber Homes—is that they trail the market by an unacceptable amount of time. In-house, your data must be fresh or it will be of little use in furthering your plan. That means a staff member with knowledge of both the real estate business and IT must be in charge of keeping the information in the company system up to the minute (however you define "minute").

That individual should also maintain the data structure so that all users can be confident of where to find what they need and how to access it. Often, we err on the IT side and allow the techies to drive the process. Their natural instinct is to play with the system. That's unacceptable. Change your structure as little as possible.

A final and very important note on managing data: The users will determine the value of the data. If they find a new way to use information that is of value to them, the system should accommodate that use. It's the college pathway theory of information: On college campuses, the students make the walkways; the paving crews later ratify their habits. You need to maintain as much flexibility in use as possible, consistent with the basic standards of management.

USING INFORMATION TO SURVIVE

Throughout this book, we have talked about the use of data. You use data to operate, manage, change, measure, and enable your business. In his recent book *Business @ the Speed of Thought,* Bill Gates states in many ways that business, to survive and prosper, must manage and react at the speed of thought. Gates's book is about modernizing and overhauling businesses, but much of it is about the use of data. Not "report on my desk" data, but data that is immediately available (real-time data) and that can be used to create something actionable. This concept of real-time actionable data and real-time action is foreign to the real estate industry;

an industry with roots and processes that were created before computers and have been resistant to change.

Internet anxiety is so common it got a front cover and a feature article in *Business Week*. The crux of the article is that business people are being outpaced by customers because the customers are often more proficient on the Internet than the sellers. Taken to its logical conclusion, this means that savvy Internet consumers can render some businesses obsolete.

It's a threat that shouldn't be taken lightly. The real estate industry is not isolated from the threat of revolution from without. If you as industry leaders went to the whiteboard, marker at the ready, could you diagram the new model for success in the real estate industry, and further, can you get your company there in time to keep your place?

Real estate professionals must collect, manage, and use data to stay vital and provide continuous sustainable value to consumers. These tasks of collecting, managing, and using data will create conflict within the industry. Who has ownership of the data is a source of conflict between owners and agents. The data, which must be collected many times, comes through the agent. The agents, especially top producers, literally run businesses within businesses, and they believe their business should husband the data. If the data are not collected, stored, and mined for value and service to the consumer, that kind of innovation will come from outside the industry. The task, which must be undertaken in this important data and information-use area, demands large-scale automation and enterprise-wide cooperation. If the data currently available were collected, stored, and used, the REALTORS would be tough to compete against. That should be the goal.

Dick Purvis, Regional Director of RE/MAX for California and Hawaii, recently stated, "The greatest challenge to residential real estate is identifying and following trends, attempting to understand the future, and positioning the enterprise in the evolving business footprint." To do that, real estate professionals need to assemble and manage all the data associated with consumers' shelter needs.

EPILOGUE

We end where we began—in the suburban confines of John and Mary Jackson's home. Surrounded by technology, taking much of it for granted, John and Mary are trying to squeeze more time for their family out of their hectic lives. The question is how best to accomplish that goal. Does John buckle down and work even more hours to beef up his share of the family income? Does Mary dare take more business risks, even though the rewards are tempting? How best can they pattern their lives to build a nest egg and also have a life?

Mary's fortunes are tied to the rising and falling winds of electronic commerce. One thing is for sure: e-commerce and the world of information technology is in its infancy. That may sound strange. We have just scratched the surface of productive steps in all corners of the world's economy. Comparing the power of the Internet today to the power it's likely to have tomorrow is like comparing a stick of dynamite with the hydrogen bomb. Like the sun itself, the Net will feed upon itself, pulsating energy in all directions, entering all corners of our world.

With e-commerce there is no choice but to follow the instincts of innovation. Today, the half-life of any innovative information product is less than four years. Think about that. An oil company recently installed a state of the art research center driven by the most advanced software technology available. The new system replaced the same software used to make one of Hollywood's greatest technological triumphs, *Jurassic Park*. In the movie, cutting edge genetic innovation is used to recreate animals extinct for millions of years. For John and his colleagues the real world is just the reverse. They are using technology to revive an industry that must compete in a growing information age, and in the process, the new systems will ensure more productivity, greater rewards, and a more secure future for John's family and the real estate profession.

In this book, we've shown that how real estate professionals conduct their professional lives needs to change. And that need is urgent. Listen and heed the signals the marketplace is sending. Remember the Indians who ignored the Spanish sails. Or the story of the frog that sat in a pot of water while the heat was turned on. If the water had been hot, the frog would have jumped to safety. Instead, the water warmed slowly. When it reached a lethal temperature, it was too late for the frog to react.

Facing reality is accepting the case for change. Fred Smith wrote a paper at Harvard outlining a new fast-delivery service that he thought would be needed in a fast-paced, growing world business environment. He got a C on the paper, but went on to found Federal Express. Southwest Airlines is among the nation's most profitable carriers because it developed a system to serve the public that offers short-haul, no-frills, and lower cost. Southwest is driven by a "fun" culture that defies the conventional approach to customer service.

Former Chairman of the Joint Chiefs of Staff, General Colin Powell, recalls a meeting among Secretary of State James Baker, himself, and Mikhail Gorbachev. Their sometimes-animated conversation was about Glasnost and where it was to lead. The decisive moment came when Gorbachev said (in words to this effect), "You don't get it Powell. You must find a new enemy to fight." Colin Powell had spent his entire career fighting the Soviets. The Iron Curtain was a symbol of tyranny and oppression, a catalyst for the strength and planning of the American military machine. Colin Powell suddenly was in a different world, with different goals, that demanded a different approach.

It's not a stretch to call today's world economy a hostile and unpredictable environment. Now that seems odd, does it not? The economy is booming. Homes are snapped up as fast as they enter the market. Investment in the stock market is soaring, as are returns. Yet, the most pregnant time for change is often when an organization is doing its best. It takes leadership to see what's ahead and to take the steps needed to ensure a company or organization is ready for the future. In today's world, the defining moment for change could be tomorrow or next week. For REALTORS® it's already here.

Archimedes said, "Give me a lever . . . and a place to stand . . . and I will move the world." We believe the steps in this book are a lever to future success for real estate professionals. It's up to you to put in place the planning and the tools to carry out a game plan—a strategy—and use the tools of technology to get the job done. This is the ultimate choice for John Jackson, husband, father, and REALTOR®. It should be your choice, too.

The Proxicom Process

Proxicom uses the Proxicom Process to manage project scope and client expectations and to deliver solutions on time and on budget. The Proxicom Process offers mechanisms for rapid adoption of best practices and reinforces consistent quality across all projects. It provides for quality assurance with unit, integration, and systems testing procedures throughout design, development, and deployment to ensure quality delivery and client satisfaction. It also aggregates and replenishes the intellectual capital of Proxicom's entire organization, thereby leveraging Proxicom's cumulative experience. The company continually seeks to evolve the Proxicom Process by identifying best practices during project reviews with Proxicom's delivery teams and clients.

All of Proxicom's client engagements utilize the Proxicom Process, which Proxicom customizes to suit specific project needs. The inclusion, timing, and cost of any phase will depend on the type of solution and the scope of work. The Proxicom Process is scalable and may be used effectively for projects of all sizes. The following are the phases of the Proxicom Process:

DEFINE INTERNET STRATEGY

The scope of the Define Internet Strategy phase ranges from defining an Internet vision for the client's overall business to developing a strategy for a specific Internet solution or offering. The Internet vision is a business strategy engagement where Proxicom assesses the client's opportunities to leverage the Internet both as a technology and as a profitable business medium. The Internet vision engagement often involves Proxicom's interactive marketing discipline, which assesses market opportunities and competition. For a specific Internet solution, the Define Internet Strategy deliverable examines the strategic objectives of the solution; how its success will be measured; and how the solution will be marketed, launched, and publicized.

PLAN SOLUTION

The Plan Solution phase determines the scope and nature of the engagement and articulates the project's tactical objectives. These objectives are refined over the course of multiple working sessions with the client. This phase results in a project plan outlining tasks, deliverables, and key milestones, which are translated into a detailed contractual agreement for the next phases of the engagement. The plan includes detailed cost estimates as well as organizational roles and responsibilities for Proxicom, the client, and other parties.

DESIGN SOLUTION

The Design Solution phase uses rapid prototyping techniques in an iterative fashion to determine and refine application requirements and specifications. A multidisciplinary team works in tandem with the client to translate the business, marketing, technical, and creative requirements of the solution into a cohesive design. This phase generally has four major parts:

1. Business Requirements Definition

Requirements, which form the foundation for successful solution designs, are refined through successive iterations and collaborations with appropriate client and user constituencies.

2. Creative Design Composition

Content and information for the solution are defined and organized. The look and feel of the solution is designed in a series of detailed site flow compositions that show page content, navigation, and links. Proxicom works closely with the client to coordinate the brand image and advertising campaigns on an ongoing basis.

3. Technical Architecture Definition

The solution is analyzed from a technical viewpoint, including the development, test, and operational architectures required. The technical, application, and data architectures of the solution are documented, addressing the requirements for hardware, software, and network environments; databases; and third-party products.

4. Specification and Prototype Development

Rapid prototyping is used to construct portions of the solution. A visual prototype is used to define page style, layout, information architecture, and navigation. Functional prototypes are used to test complex processing requirements and the effectiveness of the application and data architectures. This iterative process allows the client to review and refine the application as it takes shape during the development process.

IMPLEMENT SOLUTION

The Implement Solution phase involves the further enhancement of prototypes to construct a production-ready solution by further developing and combining the prototypes. Unit, integration, and systems testing and quality assurance procedures are incorporated throughout the development process to verify that the solution conforms with the design specifications. Testing is performed across multiple browsers and environments to ensure uniform accessibility. Once the client gives final approval of the developed solution, Proxicom works with the client through installation and rollout. This work may include system migration, data conversion, and training.

INDEX